SEX EDUCATION FOR
HUSBAND AND WIFE

WOMEN'S EMANCIPATION DURING THE PROPHET'S LIFETIME

SEX EDUCATION FOR **HUSBAND AND WIFE**

Volume 8

Abd al-Halim Abu Shuqqah

Translated and Edited by
Adil Salahi

KUBE
PUBLISHING

Sex Education for Husband and Wife, Volume 8

First published in England by
Kube Publishing Ltd
Markfield Conference Centre,
Ratby Lane, Markfield,
Leicestershire, LE67 9SY,
United Kingdom
Tel: +44 (0) 1530 249230
Email: info@ kubepublishing.com
Website: www.kubepublishing.com

WOMEN'S EMANCIPATION DURING THE PROPHET'S LIFETIME

CIP data for this book is available from the British Library.

ISBN: 978-1-84774-211-7 *Paperback*
ISBN: 978-1-84774-212-4 *Ebook*

Translate and Edit by: Adil Salahi
Cover Design by: Nasir Cadir
Typeset by: nqaddoura@hotmail.com
Printed by: Elma Printing, Turkey

Contents

Transliteration Table vii

CHAPTER I: Primary Observations 1

The Islamic Concept of Virtuous Human Life 2

CHAPTER II: Sex Education and Shyness 17

One: The reality of excessive shyness 17
Two: Proper shyness is consistent with the Qur'an and the Sunnah 20
Three: No shyness should prevent requesting or providing sex education 23
Four: Enjoying sex unlawfully 30
Five: Hadith texts with an element of sex education 32
Hadith texts referring to women's organs 34
Hadith texts encouraging intercourse and full pleasure 37
Seeking a ruling on intercourse 38
Taking care to provide the clearest explanation 42

CHAPTER III: Acknowledgement of the Strength of Sexual Desire 51

The strong temptation of sex 52
Strong but must be faced 53
A strong urge and falling into sin 55

CHAPTER IV: Islam Facilitates Lawful Ways of Enjoying Sexual Pleasure 64
Aspects of facilitating sexual enjoyment 67

CHAPTER V: What Must Be Observed in Enjoying Sex 81
One: What to observe in lawful sex 82
Two: Manners to help in avoiding unlawful sex 85
Three: Manners to observe after committing what is forbidden 89

CHAPTER VI: Islamic Law and Aspects of Sexual Enjoyment 93
One: Misconceptions that disapprove of lawful sexual enjoyment 94
Two: The various forms of permissible sexual pleasure are rewardable for both man and wife 98
Three: Love and sexual enjoyment are mutually complementary 100
Different levels of sexual enjoyment 105

CHAPTER VII: The Prophet's Guidance on Marriage and Enjoyment 113
Foreword: Why are we too sensitive about the Prophet's enjoyment of sex? 114
Striking a balance between enjoyable marriage and aspiration for the best 115
Aspiring to what is best in worship 120
The choice the Prophet offered his wives 126
Special privileges for Prophets: a continuous and miraculous tradition 128
The Prophet's special privileges in marriage and enjoyment 129
How the Prophet Enjoyed Sex 134

Transliteration Table

Consonants. Arabic

initial, unexpressed, medial and final: ء ʾ

ا	a	د	d	ض	ḍ	ك	k
ب	b	ذ	dh	ط	ṭ	ل	l
ت	t	ر	r	ظ	ẓ	م	m
ث	th	ز	z	ع	ʿ	ن	n
ج	j	س	s	غ	gh	هـ	h
ح	ḥ	ش	sh	ف	f	و	w
خ	kh	ص	ṣ	ق	q	ي	y

Vowels, diphthongs, etc.

short:	ـَـ	a	ـِـ	i	ـُـ	u
long:	ـَـا	ā	ـُـو	ū	ـِـي	ī
diphthongs:			ـَـوْ	aw		
			ـَـىْ	ay		

CHAPTER I

Primary Observations

The Islamic Concept of Virtuous Human Life

The Islamic Concept of Virtuous Human Life

Primary Observations

From the Islamic point of view, both the rise to a sublime level of spirituality and sinking into a low depth are closely related to what a person does, whether material or spiritual. This applies to all kinds of human activity, including acts of worship such as prayer, fasting and pilgrimage, or acts of kindness such as visiting a sick person, giving advice and helping someone in distress, or what gives pleasure and joy, such as eating, drinking and sex.

Seeking a higher spiritual level when doing anything is fulfilled when two requirements are met. The first is the formulation of a good intention when one is about to do something, and the other is to consciously adhere to what God permits in doing it. God neither accepts nor rewards a believer's act of worship unless these two requirements are met. He does not approve of, or reward an act of pleasure a believer does without the fulfilment of these two requirements.

Sex is one of the normal actions a person engages in. Therefore, it must be done within what God permits, seeking only a lawful partner. A Muslim should also be keen to observe the proper manners in the satisfaction of desire. It is important to ensure that the woman has her pleasure, just like the man has his. The fulfilment of sexual pleasure gives some spiritual benefits, including making it easier for a person to lower their gaze and maintain chastity, as well as feeling comfortable within oneself.

Saʿd ibn Abi Waqqāṣ narrated that the Prophet visited him when he was ill in Makkah... [The Prophet] said to him: 'Whatever you spend is counted as a charity you have given, even including a bite you place in your wife's mouth....' [Related by al-Bukhari and Muslim] Imam Ibn Ḥajar said: 'It is so, because when a permissible action is intended to please God, it becomes an act of obedience of God.'

Abu Dharr narrated that God's Messenger (peace be upon him) said: '...And [you earn the reward of] a charity in your intercourse.' People said: 'Messenger of God, would any of us fulfil his desire and still earn a reward for it?' The Prophet said: 'Would he not incur a sin if he does that in an unlawful way?' They said: 'Yes, he does.' The Prophet said: 'Likewise, when he does it in the lawful way, he earns a reward.' [Related by Muslim]

Marriage: The Point of Entry to Sex Education

The aims of marriage and the rulings and manners associated with it constitute the entry point to Islamic sex education. Imam al-Ghazālī said:

> Marriage is a good help in the fulfilment of religious duties. It humiliates devils and fortifies a person against God's enemy, Satan. It is also a means to increasing the numbers of the Muslim community, which will make the Prophet proud among other prophets. Therefore, it should

be seriously sought, with clear adherence to its values and proper understanding of its aims and purposes. Among God's fine acts is that He created man from water and established for him bonds of lineage and marriage. He planted in His creation a desire that forces them to seek the means of procreation, so as to keep the human race in existence. He then assigned honour to legitimacy, forbidding adultery and showing its ugly picture so as to make people turn away from it. He made its practice a serious and ghastly offence, while He encouraged legitimate marriage.'

God says: 'Marry the single from among you.' (24: 32). This is an order to the community to facilitate the marriage of single people. He also says: 'Do not prevent your women from marrying their husbands if they have agreed with each other in a fair manner.' (2: 232) This is a prohibition order against stopping proper marriage. The Prophet said: 'Whoever turns away from my practice does not belong to me.' He also said: 'Marriage is my practice. Whoever likes my nature should follow my practice.' 'Umar said: 'Nothing stops marriage except disability or a preference of evil ways.' Ibn 'Abbās said: 'No one's worship is complete until he gets married.'

One of the Prophet's Companions devoted himself to his service, even staying close at night so that he would be available whenever the Prophet needed something. One day the Prophet said to him: 'Do you not want to get married?' He said: 'Messenger of God, I am poor and I have nothing. Besides, I would not be serving you.' The Prophet did not say anything to him. Later, the Prophet said the same thing and he gave the same answer. Then the man reflected, and he said to himself: 'God's Messenger is certainly better aware than me of what is best for me in this life and in the life to come, and what will help me to draw closer to God. If he asks me a third time, I shall do as he says.' The Prophet said to him again: 'Will you not get married?' He answered: 'Messenger of God, help me get married.' The Prophet said: 'Go to those people [naming a certain clan] and say: "God's Messenger bids you to marry me to your daughter."' The man said: 'Messenger of God, I have nothing.' The Prophet said to his Companions: 'Collect for your brother the equivalent of the weight of a date stone in gold.' They did this and took him to those people who gave him their daughter in marriage. The Prophet told him to give a wedding dinner. The Prophet's Companions provided him with a sheep for this purpose.

Marriage is a time-honoured practice and one which all prophets upheld. It gives five beneficial results: begetting children, satisfying desire, managing one's home, increasing one's people and self-discipline.

The first benefit is begetting children. This is the main purpose for which marriage is legislated. The aim is to keep up procreation so that the world will always be populated by humans. The sexual desire is an urge to fulfil this purpose. Having children serves four aspects of drawing closer to God. The first and most important aspect is that it helps man to contemplate the fine work of God and how His purpose is fulfilled by His will... The second aspect is seeking to please God's Messenger (peace be upon him) by increasing the object that gives him pride. He has stated this very clearly saying: 'Marry a motherly and friendly woman, as I want to have the largest community.' [Related by al-Nasā'ī] The third aspect is that a parent may leave behind a good child who prays for his or her parents. The Prophet mentions in a hadith that when a person dies all their actions come to an end except in three ways, and one of these is a good child. In any case, a believer's supplication for parents is useful, regardless of the status of the supplicant. A parent is rewarded for they child's supplication, because the child is part of what he gain in this life, and the parent is not accountable for the child's bad deeds, because no one bears responsibility for another person's deeds. The fourth aspect is when a child dies before the parent. The Prophet said: 'If any Muslim suffers the death of three children, he will not be touched by the Fire except for the fulfilment of the oath.' [Related by al-Bukhari and Muslim] Another version of this hadith is related by Ahmad and narrated Maḥmūd ibn Asad from Jābir, adds the following: 'We said: "Messenger of God, how about two?" He said: "And two." Maḥmūd ibn Asad said: 'I said to Jābir: I think that had you said: "and one", he would have said, "and one." Jābir said: I, too, think so.' The Prophet said: 'Children who die young are the young dwellers of Heaven. Each of them receives its parent, or he said parents, and holds his robe, or he said: his hand, as I would hold the edge of your robe... and will not let go until God has admitted it and its parent into Heaven.' [Related by Muslim]

The second benefit is fortification against Satan and satisfaction of desire while lowering one's gaze and maintaining chastity. It is to this that the Prophet (peace be upon him) refers when he says: 'Whoever gets married fortifies half of his faith. Let him fear God in what he does with the other half.' Again the reference is to marriage in his advice: 'Whoever of you is able to undertake the requirements of marriage should do so... Whoever is unable may resort to fasting, as it weakens desire.'

The third benefit is the comfort it gives through sitting with one's wife and having fun with her. This enables a person to be relaxed and attentive to his worship.

The fourth benefit is home management, because a good wife attends to her home and sets it on the right footing. As such, she helps to strengthen her husband in his faith.

The fifth benefit is self-discipline, as a man needs to take care of his wife and family, attend to their needs and provide what is due to them.[1]

Marriage: a Social Institution for Sexual Pleasure

Marriage is an aspect of sound human nature and a practice of all prophets and messengers of God (peace be upon them all). God says: 'God has given you spouses of your own kind and has given you, through your spouses, children and grandchildren, and provided you with wholesome sustenance.' (16: 72) He also says: 'We have indeed sent messengers before you and given them wives and offspring.' (13: 38)

Marriage is also a practice recommended by Prophet Muhammad (peace be upon him). He was sent with the message that complements and perfects all laws given to earlier prophets. He set good manners and moral values at the level of perfection, so that natural desires and the practice of prophets remain well preserved. He started all this with encouraging marriage. God says: 'If you fear that you may not deal fairly by the orphans, you may marry of other women as may be agreeable to you, two or three or four. But if you fear that you will not be able to maintain fairness between them, then marry only one.' (4: 3) 'Abdullāh ibn Mas'ūd said: 'God's Messenger (peace be upon

1. Al-Ghazālī, *Iḥyā' 'Ulūm al-Dīn*, Vol. 2, pp. 688-709. (Summarized).

him) said to us: 'Young men, whoever of you is able to undertake the requirements of marriage should do so. [Marriage] helps to lower one's gaze and maintain chastity. Whoever is unable may resort to fasting, as it weakens desire.' [Related by al-Bukhari and Muslim]

When the Prophet noted an inclination towards hardship on the part of some of his Companions, with one of them intending to abstain from marriage, seeking to imitate the celibacy of Christian priests, he gave a clear warning. Anas ibn Mālik narrated: 'Three men came to the Prophet's homes enquiring from his wives about his worship at home. When they were told the details, they appeared to think that it was less than what is adequate. They said to each other: "Our position is far below that of the Prophet. He has been forgiven all his sins, past, present and future." One of them said: "I will pray all night every night for the rest of my life." The second said: "I will fast every day without fail." The third said: "As for me, I will never marry." The Prophet went to them and said: "Are you the ones who said so and so? By God, I am the most God-fearing person among you, yet I fast some days and do not fast on others, and I pray at night but I also sleep, and I do marry. Such is my tradition and anyone who does not follow my tradition does not belong to me."' [Related by al-Bukhari and Muslim]

Sa'd ibn Abi Waqqāṣ said: 'The Prophet refused 'Uthmān's ibn Maẓ'ūn's suggestion. Had he agreed to his request of celibacy, we would have emasculated ourselves.' [Related by al-Bukhari and Muslim] What is meant by the 'request of celibacy' in this context is refraining from marriage and what it involves of satisfying desire, in order to devote oneself to worship. The Prophet wanted to urge young people to endeavour to get married, giving them the promise that their effort will be successful. Abu Hurayrah reports that God's Messenger (peace be upon him) said: 'Three people earn God's help by right: the one who strives for God's cause, and the slave who has contracted to buy his own freedom and wants to pay, and the one who seeks marriage to maintain his chastity.' [Related by al-Tirmidhī]

A Wholesome Pleasure in This Life

Islam considers sexual pleasure as one of the good things of this life and looks at it as one of its pleasant enjoyments. Good believers are promised to have all these enjoyments available to them in a perfect way in the life to come. God says: 'Say, 'Who is there to forbid the beauty which God has produced for His servants, and the wholesome means of sustenance?' Say, 'They are [lawful] in the life of this world, to all who believe – to be theirs alone on the Day of Resurrection.' Thus do We make Our revelations clear to people of knowledge.' (7: 32) 'They will abide in all that their souls have ever desired.' (21: 102) 'We are your guardians in the life of this world and in the life to come. There you shall have all that your souls desire, and all that you ask for.' (41: 31) 'There will be found all that the souls may desire and the eyes may delight in.' (43: 71)

Numerous Qur'anic verses state in superior language the great enjoyments God will grant to His pious servants in the life to come. The following are some of these verses which include references to sexual pleasure. God says: 'You, servants of Mine, no fear need you have today, nor shall you grieve. You, who have believed in Our revelations and surrendered yourselves to Us, enter paradise, you and your spouses, in pure happiness." (43: 68-70)

'Those who are destined for paradise are today happily occupied. Together with their spouses, they will be in shady groves seated on soft couches.' (36: 55-56)

'To those who believe and do good deeds give the good tidings that they shall reside in gardens through which running waters flow. Whenever they are offered fruits therefrom, they say, 'We have been given the same before', for they shall be provided with what looks similar. They shall also have pure spouses and they shall reside there for ever.' (2: 25)

'Say: shall I tell you of better things than these? For the God-fearing there are, with their Lord, gardens through which running waters flow where they shall dwell forever, and spouses of perfect chastity, and God's good pleasure. God is mindful of His servants.' (3: 15)

'But those who believe and do righteous deeds We shall admit into gardens through which running waters flow, where they shall abide beyond the count of time. There they shall have pure spouses, and We shall admit them into a cool, dense shade.' (4: 57)

'The God-fearing will certainly be in a safe position, amid gardens and fountains, wearing garments of silk and brocade, facing one another. Thus shall it be. And We shall pair them with pure companions with most beautiful eyes.' (44: 51-54)

The believers will be in gardens and in bliss, rejoicing in all that their Lord will have granted them; for their Lord will have warded off from them the suffering of the blazing Fire. "Eat and drink with healthy enjoyment as a reward for what you have done." They will recline on couches arranged in rows, and We shall pair them with companions having most beautiful eyes.' (52: 17-20)

'Theirs shall be a predetermined sustenance: fruits; and they will be honoured in gardens of bliss, seated on soft couches, facing one another. A cup will be passed round among them with a drink from a flowing spring: clear, delicious to those who drink it, causing no headiness or intoxication. With them will be mates of modest gaze, most beautiful of eye, as if they were hidden eggs.' (37: 41-49)

'Let all this be a reminder. The God-fearing will certainly have a good place to return to: gardens of perpetual bliss, with gates wide open to them. They will be comfortably seated there, and they will call for abundant fruit and drink, having beside them well-matched mates of modest gaze.' (38: 49-52)

‘They will recline on carpets lined with rich brocade; and the fruit of both these gardens will be within easy reach. Which, then, of your Lord’s blessings do you both deny? In both [gardens] will be mates of modest gaze, whom neither man nor jinn will have touched before. Which, then, of your Lord’s blessings do you both deny? [These mates look] like rubies and corals.’ (55: 54-58)

‘There will be in [these gardens] all things most excellent and beautiful. Which, then, of your Lord’s blessings do you both deny? [They will have] dark-eyed and modest companions, sheltered in pavilions. Which, then, of your Lord’s blessings do you both deny? Neither man nor jinn will have touched them before.’ (55: 70-74)

‘There will be for them companions with large beautiful eyes, like hidden pearls, a reward for what they used to do.’ (56: 22-24)

‘We will have brought forth [their mates] in perfect creation, making them virgins, full of love, of matching age, for those on the right.’ (56: 35-38)

‘The God-fearing shall have a place of security, gardens and vineyards and high-bosomed maidens, of equal age, for companions.’ (78: 31-33)

Abu Hurayrah said that God’s Messenger (peace be upon him) said: ‘God says: I have prepared for My devoted servants what no eye has seen, no ear has heard of, and no human has ever imagined. Read, if you will: “No one can imagine what blissful delights have been kept in store for them.”’ (32: 17)

Abu Hurayrah said that God’s Messenger (peace be upon him) said: ‘The first group to enter Heaven will look like a full moon. They neither spit, blow their noses nor defecate there. Their utensils are of gold, their combs are of gold and silver; their brazier is perfumed wood; their perspiration is musk. Every one of them has two wives, so pretty that the marrow of their leg bones is visible behind their flesh. No conflict or hatred is felt by them. Their hearts are like the heart of one person. They glorify God morning and evening.'

'Abdullāh ibn Qays al-Ash'arī narrates from his father that the Prophet (peace be upon him) said: 'The tent is a hollowed pearl in the sky, and it is thirty miles long. In every corner of it, a believer has a family which is unseen by the others.' [Related by al-Bukhari and Muslim]

Anas ibn Mālik said that God's Messenger (peace be upon him) said: 'There is a marketplace in Heaven and its people go there every Friday. A northerly wind blows touching their faces and clothes. They increase in beauty and fine appearance. They go back to their families more beautiful and more good-looking. Their families say to them: "By God, since we last saw you, you have increased in beauty and fine appearance." They reply: "And you, too, have increased in beauty and fine appearance since we last saw you."' [Related by Muslim]

Anas reports: "Ḥārithah, a young lad, was killed in the Battle of Badr. His mother came to the Prophet and said to him: 'Messenger of God! You know how dear to me Ḥārithah was. If he is in Heaven, I will bear my bereavement with patience. If it is the opposite, then you shall see what I will do?' The Prophet said to her: 'Bless you! Have you lost your mind? Do you think it is one heaven? There are many heavens and he is in Paradise.'" [Related by al-Bukhari] The Prophet also said: "Undertaking a march in the morning or the evening, for God's sake, is better than this world and all it contains. A very small place, or the length of anyone's foot in Heaven is better than this world and all it contains. Should one woman from Heaven look at the earth, she would lighten the entire space in between them and fill it with fine smell. Her headdress is better than this world and all it contains." [Related by al-Bukhari]

Recommendations for Parents on Sexual Guidance for Their Children[2]

- Parents should read some books of sex education in order to acquire good insight into it. It is also advantageous to attend seminars that bring together medical doctors and specialists in psychology and sociology.
- Complete silence on this subject does not help in keeping the child on the right way. On the contrary, it opens a gate for wrong information from unreliable sources, such as friends, servants or unscientific books.
- Offering the necessary information related to sex, at the right time, in the right measure and an appropriate way, without embarrassment or sensitivity. Parents should gently answer every question a child asks.
- A child, boy or girl, may uncover its private parts, or touch and fondle them. Children may fondle each other's private parts. All this may happen casually as a child likes to discover the various parts of its body, or the body of another child. Moreover, such fondling gives a light sense of pleasure. When this happens, parents should kindly speak to the child, in the same way as they teach a child the proper behaviour when eating or speaking to people. There must be no sensitivity that makes the child feel that it did something wrong. It may be better to gently direct the child's attention to some other thing of interest.
- When the child approaches puberty, it is important to present some necessary information. It may be useful to choose an appropriate occasion. The information provided should be put in a framework of the story of life and that it begins with the meeting of a male and female, and that this applies to plants, animals and humans. A parent may draw the child's

2. These are mere thoughts on a serious matter. Parents should refer to specialized books. - Author's note.

attention to a plant and speak about the function of flowers and pollination. Alternatively, reference may be made to an animal, such as a cat, so that the conversation will be smooth and simple, as applies to anything that we may come across in our daily life. God says: 'All things We have created in pairs, so that you may take thought.' (49: 49)

- After puberty, which is often called adolescence, the parents should ensure a proper family atmosphere to help their son and daughter go through this period without difficulty or problems. This may include:

  i. Providing some occasions for mixed meetings within the family, observing the standards of propriety, so that such meetings are felt to be natural, giving neither boy nor girl any embarrassment when they need to meet.
  ii. Encouraging adolescents to participate in different activities, whether sport, art, educational or social, etc. In most cases, involvement in such activities reduces sexual urges.
  iii. When either parent, or both, intends to do some voluntary fasting, they should encourage their adolescent child to join them, because fasting also cools the sexual urge.
  iv. Children should have ample opportunity for their play and have friends of similar age. They should not have friends who are either considerably older or younger, so as to guard against the elder abusing the younger, or the younger presenting the elder with the wrong temptation. In this respect, parents' guidance should be positive, preceded by providing the opportunity for the child to meet and play with other children of similar age.
  v. When children approach puberty, they must be separated in their sleeping areas, so that girls have their own

room and boys their room. If this is not possible, each should have a separate bed, or at least each child should have their own cover.

vi. Ensuring safety for children: they must not be exposed to frequent and private conversations with servants, or with relatives or neighbours who are either considerably older or younger than them.

- Strengthening the father's ties with his sons and the mother's with her daughters to develop an intellectual and psychological bond between them to help mutual understanding, and to express their thoughts and ask their questions. Thus, children will be able to speak about any social or sexual problems they may experience.
- A parent may refer on some occasion to the practice of masturbation. He states that Islamic scholars and medical doctors agree that it should occur only when there is pressing need, and in moderation. Otherwise, it weakens a person and causes distraction and depression. It is better to occupy oneself with some useful hobby or activity.

CHAPTER II

Sex Education and Shyness

- One: The reality of excessive shyness
- Two: Proper shyness is consistent with the Qur'an and the Sunnah
- Three: No shyness should prevent requesting or providing sex education
- Four: Enjoying sex unlawfully
- Five: Hadith texts with an element of sex education
- Hadith texts referring to women's organs
- Hadith texts encouraging intercourse and full pleasure
- Seeking a ruling on intercourse
- Taking care to provide the clearest explanation

Sex Education and Shyness

One: The reality of excessive shyness

We have inherited a misconception that modesty requires that a Muslim must never be party to any discussion of any matter related to sex. It has been instilled as part of our upbringing that a Muslim should avoid any reference to this subject. No question should be asked even to seek much needed information, and no answer should be given when required. No involvement in any such discussion should occur, no matter how serious and important. In the light of this misconception, the entire subject of sex remains hidden behind thick walls and heavy curtains that cannot be penetrated except by one who is impudently daring, carelessly frivolous or totally deprived of morality.

Good mannered and well brought up people in Muslim communities are in a strange position. If a serious discussion touches upon an element of sex, you will find them blushing and stammering, as though they feel themselves to be in a compromising position and they are eager to steer away from it. If an elder, a parent or a teacher takes the initiative in order to give advice on some point of sex, an expression of disapproval will be on the faces of their audience and they may say within themselves: 'He should better stop.' They may even turn away or divert the discussion along some other alley. If they find themselves compelled to listen, they do so with aversion, as though the subject jars on their ears. If some discussion is urgently needed, it should only take place in whispers and very privately, as though they are doing something shameful that must remain hidden from onlookers and eavesdroppers. Moreover, the discussion should have a long preamble before the subject matter itself is embarrassingly tackled. Everyone of the interlocutors has to exert a hard effort before they can express themselves plainly.

If a young man or a young woman faces a problem related to sex or to genitalia, they do not know to whom to turn for advice, or where they can have a proper solution or treatment. Should he talk to either parent, or to a teacher, friend or servant? In many cases, the subject is first approached with a servant, because it is easiest. Moreover, talking to a friend is easier than talking to a parent or a teacher. The reason is that those elders have placed a barrier between themselves and their children and students. This barrier is inadvertently erected through long years of silence about this subject, and their rebuke of their young children when they put forward some innocent questions about sex. Thus, young children get the feeling that whatever is related to sex is shameful and must not be discussed. Indeed, modesty requires that one steers far away from it. Thus, well brought up children and young men and women have come to prefer silence over raising a question about sex, even though such silence has serious effects and a discussion may be fruitful in overcoming a problem or treating a difficulty.

In short, excessive shyness is merely a psychological situation that has established deep roots in our community, making it difficult to treat and overcome. It is the result of old and flimsy misconceptions that have no basis in Islam. Yet we have inherited these through several generations, as though they are a part of faith that we must continue to uphold. We do not seem to realize that we have unnecessarily burdened ourselves, following our own desires in opposition to God's law, the guidance of the Prophet and the practice of his Companions.

Two: Proper shyness is consistent with the Qur'an and the Sunnah

Abu Hurayrah narrated that the Prophet (peace be upon him) said: 'Faith has sixty-odd aspects, and modesty is an aspect of faith.' [Related by al-Bukhari and Muslim] 'Abdullāh ibn 'Umar narrated that God's Messenger (peace be upon him) passed by a man from the Anṣār who was admonishing his brother about his shyness. The Prophet said to him: 'Leave him alone; for shyness is a part of faith.' [Related by al-Bukhari and Muslim] 'Abdullāh ibn Mas'ūd narrated that the Prophet (peace be upon him) said: 'Among the words people have retained from the early prophethood is: If you feel no shame, then do as you wish.' [Related by al-Bukhari and Muslim]

'Imrān ibn Ḥuṣayn quoted the Prophet as saying: 'Modesty brings nothing but good.' Bushayr ibn Ka'b said: 'It is written in al-Ḥikmah that it imparts respectability and serenity.' 'Imrān said: 'I am relating to you what God's Messenger said and you tell me about your books!' [Related by al-Bukhari and Muslim]

Shyness which leads to loss of rights is not what Islam recommends. That sort of attitude betrays shame and disability. What Islam praises and advises every Muslim to have is the moral value that motivates a person to steer away from what is foul. Thābit al-Bunānī narrated: 'I was visiting Anas and one of his daughters was present. Anas said: "A woman came to the Prophet (peace be upon him) offering herself [as a wife] to him. She said: 'Messenger of God, will you accept me?'

[In another version, she said: Messenger of God, I have come to offer myself as a present to you] Anas's daughter said: "How impolite! What a shame! What a shame!" Anas said: "She is better than you. She wished to marry the Prophet and she offered herself to him."' [Related by al-Bukhari]

Here is an example of proper modesty related in the Qur'an: 'One of the two women then came back to him, walking shyly, and said: "My father invites you, so that he might duly reward you for having watered our flock for us."' (28: 25) This is the case of a young woman going out to meet a stranger. It is perfectly proper that she should experience a feeling of shyness. Had her shyness stopped her from going out to meet this person, when such a meeting was likely to bring about some benefit, then it would have been a negative and improper shyness.

The following hadiths provide examples of proper modesty: 'Ā'ishah narrated that Asmā' bint Shakal asked the Prophet about the bath necessary after menstruation. He said: "Any woman of you should take her water and *sidr* and perform the complete ablution [i.e. wudu]. She then pours water over her head and rubs it well so as to penetrate to the skin of her head. She then pours water over her body. Then she takes a piece of cotton, perfumed with musk, and cleanses herself with it." Asmā' said: "How does she cleanse herself with it?" The Prophet said: "All glory be to God! Cleanse yourself with it." 'Ā'ishah said (as though to keep it secret): "Follow the traces of blood." She then asked him about taking a bath to remove the state of ceremonial impurity. He said: "She takes water and performs the ablution well, or complete, then pours water over her head and rubs it so as to reach the skin of her head. She then pours water over her body." 'Ā'ishah said: "Good women are the Anṣār women. Modesty has not prevented them from learning about their religion."' [Related by al-Bukhari and Muslim. This is Muslim's version]

ʿAlī ibn Abu Ṭālib reports: 'I used to discharge *madhī*,[3] but I was too shy to ask God's Messenger about it (another version adds: because of his daughter's position). I requested al-Miqdād ibn al-Aswad and he asked him. The Prophet said: "It requires ablution, i.e. wudu."' [Related by al-Bukhari and Muslim]

Umm Salamah narrated: 'Umm Sulaym came to see God's Messenger and said: 'Messenger of God, shyness should not prevent the truth. Should a woman have a full bath if she has a wet dream?' The Prophet said: 'Yes, if she has a discharge.' Umm Salamah covered her face and said: 'Messenger of God, does a woman have a wet dream?' He said: 'Yes, indeed. What else explains that her child looks after her?' [Related by al-Bukhari and Muslim]

Abu Mūsā narrated: 'Some of the Muhājirīn and the Anṣār differed on this point. The Anṣār people said: "A bath is due only if the man ejaculates", but the Muhājirīn said: "It is due in the case of touch." Abu Mūsā said: "I shall bring you the right answer. I stood up and sought admission to ʿĀ'ishah. I was given permission. I said to her: 'Mother', or 'Mother of the Believers, I want to ask you about something but I feel shy.' She said: 'Do not be ashamed to put to me a question you would have asked your mother who gave birth to you. I am also your mother.' I said: 'What makes a bath required?' She said: 'You are asking the expert. God's Messenger (peace be upon him) said: "If the man sits between her four limbs and the two genitals are in touch, a bath is obligatory."' [Related by Muslim]

However, proper modesty requires that two situations related to sexual matters must not be talked about. The first is what a married couple do with each other in their bedroom, and the other is trifling and joking about matters related to sexual pleasure.

---

3. *Madhī* is a thin liquid that a man may discharge during foreplay. ʿAlī meant that he often had such discharge. – Author's note.

Three: No shyness should prevent requesting or providing sex education.

1. MAN'S CREATION

Numerous verses of the Qur'an include an aspect of sex education. Many of these refer to the creation of man, starting with the man's sperm. God says: 'Indeed, We create man out of the essence of clay, then We place him, a gamete, in a safe place of rest. Then We create out of the gamete a clinging cell mass, and out of the clinging cell mass We create an embryo. Then We create within the embryo bones, then We clothe the bones with flesh. We then bring this into being as another creation. Exalted be God, the best of creators.' (23: 12-14) 'It is He who creates you out of dust, then out of a gamete, then out of a clinging cell mass; and then He brings you forth as infants. He then lets you reach maturity, and then grow old.' (40: 67) 'Perish man! How ungrateful he is! Of what did God create him? Of a drop of sperm. He created him and proportioned him. He makes his path smooth for him.' (80: 17-20)

Other verses speak about man originating with a 'humble fluid', which is man's semen and how it is discharged: 'He begins the creation of man out of clay; then He causes his progeny to be begotten out of the essence of a humble fluid.' (32: 7-8) 'Have We not created you from a humble fluid, placing it in a safe lodging?' (77: 20-21) 'It is He who creates the two sexes, male and female, from a seed as it is lodged in place.' (53: 45-46) 'Does man think that he will be left without purpose? Was he not a mere drop of emitted sperm? It then became a clinging cell mass, and then God created and shaped it, fashioning out of it the two sexes, male and female.' (75: 36-39) 'Consider the semen you discharge: do you create it, or are We the Creator?' (56: 58-59) 'Let man then reflect: of what he is created. He is created of gushing water. He issues from in between the loins and the chest bones.' (86: 5-7)

2. Natural attraction

Many verses in the Qur'an refer to the natural mutual attraction between men and women. God says: 'Alluring to man is the enjoyment of worldly desires through women and offspring, heaped-up treasures of gold and silver, horses of high mark, cattle and plantations. These are the comforts of this life. With God is the best of all goals.' (3: 14)

'You will incur no sin if you give a hint of a marriage offer to [widowed] women or keep such an intention to yourselves. God knows that you will entertain such intentions concerning them. Do not, however, plight your troth in secret; but speak only in a decent manner.' (2: 235)

'She in whose house he was living tried to seduce him. She bolted the doors and said, 'Come.' He said: 'God protect me. Goodly has my master made my stay here. Those who do wrong come to no good.' She truly desired him, and he desired her. [He would have succumbed] had he not seen a clear sign of his Lord. Thus We averted from him evil and indecency. He was truly one of Our faithful servants.' (12: 23-24)

'In the city, women were saying: "This minister's wife is trying to seduce her slave boy, as she is passionately in love with him. We see that she is clearly going astray." When she heard of their malicious talk, she sent for them, and prepared for them a sumptuous repast, and handed each one of them a knife and said [to Joseph]: "Come out and present yourself to them." When they saw him, they were amazed at him, and they cut their hands, exclaiming: "God preserve us! This is no mortal man! This is none other than a noble angel." Said she: "This is he on whose account you have been blaming me! Indeed I have tried to seduce him, but he guarded his chastity. Now, however, if he does not do what I bid him, he shall certainly be thrown in prison, and shall indeed be humiliated."' (12: 30-32)

3. Genitalia

Some verses of the Qur'an refer to people's private parts and the nakedness of exposing them. God says about Satan's seduction of Adam: 'And [as for you], Adam: dwell you and your wife in this Garden, and eat, both of you, whatever you may desire; but do not come near this tree, lest you become wrongdoers.' But Satan whispered to them both, so that he might show them their nakedness, of which they had previously been unaware. He said to them: "Your Lord has only forbidden you this tree lest you two become angels or immortals." And he swore to them: "I am indeed giving you sound advice." Thus he cunningly deluded them. And when they both had tasted the fruit of the tree, their nakedness became apparent to them, and they began to cover themselves with leaves from the Garden. Their Lord called out to them: "Did I not forbid you that tree and tell you both that Satan is your open enemy?"' (7: 19-22)

The following two verses include a reference to children attaining puberty and how this should affect their social behaviour. God says: 'Believers! Let those whom you rightfully possess, and those of you who have not yet attained to puberty, ask leave of you at three times of day: before the prayer of daybreak, and whenever you lay aside your garments in the middle of the day, and after the prayer of nightfall. These are three occasions on which you may happen to be undressed. Beyond these occasions, neither you nor they will incur any sin if they move freely about you, attending to one another. Thus God makes clear to you His revelations. God is all-knowing, wise. Yet when your children attain to puberty, let them ask leave of you, as do those senior to them [in age]. Thus does God make revelations clear to you. God is all-knowing, wise.' (24: 58-59)

The Qur'an speaks about menstruation and the waiting period a woman needs to observe in the case of divorce or widowhood. Detailed rulings, concerning men and women, are given for the different situations that people may have. God says: 'As for those of your women who are beyond the age of monthly courses, as well as for those who do not have any courses, their waiting period, if you have any doubt, is three months. As for those who are with child, their waiting term shall end when they deliver their burden. For everyone who is God-fearing, God makes things easy.' (65: 4)

'They ask you about menstruation. Say: It is an unclean condition; so keep aloof from women during menstruation, and do not draw near to them until they are cleansed. When they have cleansed themselves, you may go in unto them in the proper way, as God has bidden you. God loves those who turn to Him in repentance, and He loves those who keep themselves pure.' (2: 222)

'Prophet! When you divorce women, divorce them with a view to their prescribed waiting period, and reckon the period accurately. Be conscious of God, your Lord. Do not drive them out of their homes, nor shall they themselves leave, unless they commit a flagrant indecency. These are the bounds set by God. Whoever transgresses God's bounds wrongs his own soul. You never know; after that, God may bring about some new situation.' (65: 1)

'Believers! If you marry believing women and then divorce them before the marriage is consummated, you have no reason to expect them to observe a waiting period. Hence, provide well for them and release them in a becoming manner.' (33: 49)

'Divorced women shall wait, by themselves, for three monthly courses.' (2: 228)

The Qur'an also refers to the womb as closely related to pregnancy and creation. God says: 'It is He who shapes you in the wombs as He pleases. There is no deity save Him, the Almighty, the Wise.' (3: 6)

'God knows what every female bears, and by how much the wombs may fall short [in gestation], and by how much they may increase. With Him everything has its definite measure.' (13: 8)

'It is unlawful for them to conceal what God might have created in their wombs, if they believe in God and the Last Day.' (2: 228)

The Qur'an refers to human private parts as being closely connected to maintaining chastity. God says: 'Tell believing men to lower their gaze and to be mindful of their chastity. This is most conducive to their purity. God is certainly aware of all that they do. And tell believing women to lower their gaze and to be mindful of their chastity.' (24: 30-31)

'They are mindful of their chastity except with those joined to them in marriage, or those whom they rightfully possess - for then, they are free of all blame, whereas those who seek to go beyond that [limit] are indeed transgressors.' (23: 5-7)

'All men and women who are mindful of their chastity.' (33: 35)

'And Mary, the daughter of 'Imrān, who guarded her chastity; and We breathed of Our spirit into her. She accepted the truth of her Lord's words and His revealed Books. She was truly devout.' (66: 12)

The state of ceremonial impurity is mentioned in the Qur'an in relation to prayer and the fact that such state must be removed for the prayer to be valid. God says: 'Believers, do not attempt to pray when you are drunk, [but wait] until you know what you are saying; nor when you are in a state of ceremonial impurity, except if you are on your way, until you have bathed.' (4: 43)

'Believers, when you are about to pray, wash your faces, and your hands and arms up to the elbows, and pass your wet hands lightly over your heads, and wash your feet up to the ankles. If you are in a state of ceremonial impurity, purify yourselves.' (5: 6)

4. Lawful sex

According to Islam, the lawful way to satisfy the sexual desire is within marriage. Marriage is the proper home for raising the future generation. Marriage is a strong bond and a firm covenant as Qur'anic verses describe it: 'Your wives are your tilth; go, then, to your tilth as you may desire, but first provide something for your souls. Fear God and know that you shall meet Him. Give the happy news to the believers.' (2: 223)

Intimacy between husband and wife and foreplay are referred to in the Qur'an: 'It is lawful for you to be intimate with your wives during the night preceding the fast. They are as a garment for you, as you are for them. God is aware that you have been deceiving yourselves in this respect, and He has turned to you in His mercy and pardoned you. So, you may now lie with them and seek what God has ordained for you. Eat and drink until you can see the white streak of dawn against the blackness of the night. Then resume the fast till nightfall. Do not lie with your wives when you are in retreat in the mosques.' (2: 187)

'The pilgrimage takes place in the months appointed for it. Whoever undertakes the pilgrimage in those months shall, while on pilgrimage, abstain from sex, all wicked conduct and wrangling.' (2: 197)

Qur'anic verses refer to sexual intercourse and its enjoyment in an elegant way, as God says: 'If you wish to take one wife in place of another and you have given the first one a large dowry, do not take away anything of it. Would you take it away though that constitutes a gross injustice and a manifest sin? How can you take it away when each of you has been privy with the other, and they have received from you a most solemn pledge?' (4: 20-21)

'Forbidden to you [in marriage] are your mothers, your daughters, your sisters, your aunts paternal and maternal, your brother's daughters and your sister's daughters, your mothers who have given suck to you, your suckling sisters, the mothers of your wives, your stepdaughters - who are your foster children - born to your wives with whom you have consummated your marriage; but if you have not consummated your marriage with them, you will incur no sin [by marrying their daughters], and the wives of your own begotten sons; and [you are forbidden] to have two sisters as your wives at one and the same time, unless it be a thing of the past. God is much-forgiving, ever-merciful.' (4: 23)

'But if you are ill, or travelling, or if one of you has come from the toilet, or if you have cohabited with your wife and can find no water, then have recourse to pure dust.' (4: 43)

Said she [i.e. Mary]: 'My Lord, How can I have a son when no man has ever touched me?' [The angel] answered: 'Thus it is. God creates what He wills. When He wills a thing to be, He only says to it 'Be', and it is.' (3: 47)

'You will incur no sin if you divorce women before having touched them or settled a dowry for them. Provide for them, the rich according to his means and the straitened according to his means. Such a provision, in an equitable manner, is an obligation binding on the righteous. If you divorce them before having touched them but after having settled a dowry for them, then give them half of that which you have settled, unless they forgo it or he in whose hand is the marriage tie forgoes it. To forgo what is due to you is closer to being righteous. Do not forget to act benevolently to one another. God sees all that you do.' (2: 236-237)

'Those who separate themselves from their wives by saying, 'You are as unlawful to me as my mother', and then go back on what they have said, must atone by freeing a slave before the couple may resume their full marital relations. This is an admonition to you, and God is fully aware of all that you do. However, he who does not have the means shall fast instead for two consecutive months before the couple may resume their full marital relations; and he who is unable to do so shall feed sixty needy people; this, so that you may prove your faith in God and His Messenger. Such are the bounds set by God. Painful suffering awaits those who will not believe.' (58: 3-4)

Four: Enjoying Sex Unlawfully

The Qur'an mentions the opposite way, which is to seek sexual pleasure in unlawful ways. It condemns fornication and adultery in clear terms. God says: 'As for the adulteress and the adulterer, flog each of them with a hundred stripes, and let not compassion for them keep you from [carrying out] this law of God, if you truly believe in God and the Last Day; and let a number of believers witness their punishment. The adulterer couples with none other than an adulteress or an idolatress; and with the adulteress couples none other than an adulterer or an idolater. This is forbidden to the believers.' (24: 2-3)

'And who never invoke any deity side by side with God, and do not take any human being's life – [the life] which God has willed to be sacred – except for a just cause, and do not commit adultery. Whoever does any of this will face punishment.' (25: 68)

The Qur'an always refers to sex outside the bond of marriage as *fāḥishah* which may translated as 'gross indecency' or 'immoral conduct.' God says: 'As for those of your women who are guilty of gross immoral conduct, call upon four from among you to bear witness against them. If they so testify, then confine the guilty women to their houses until death takes them or God opens another way for them.' (4: 15)

'If after their marriage,[4] they are guilty of gross immoral conduct, they shall be liable to half the penalty to which free women are liable. This provision applies to those of you who fear to stumble into sin. Yet it is better for you to be patient. God is much-forgiving, ever-merciful.' (4: 25)

The Qur'an condemns homosexuality in clear terms, citing the case of Lot's people as example, and refers to it in several surahs with very similar terms. Here is an example: 'And Lot said to his people: Will you persist in the indecencies none in all the world had ever committed before you? With lust you approach men instead of women. Indeed, you are given to excesses.' (7: 80-81)

It also condemns adultery, whether committed in secret or openly. God makes clear that even with slave women sex is permissible only within marriage. He says: 'Marry them, then, with their people's consent and give them their dowries in an equitable manner, as chaste women who give themselves in honest wedlock, not in fornication, nor as women who have secret love companions.' (4: 25)

'Today, all the good things of life have been made lawful to you. The food of those who were given revelations is lawful to you, and your food is lawful to them. And the virtuous women from among the believers and the virtuous women from among those who were given revelations before you [are also lawful to you] when you give them their dowries, taking them in honest wedlock, not in fornication, nor as mistresses. Anyone who rejects the faith [will find that] all his works will be in vain. In the life to come he shall be among the losers.' (5: 5)

Reference to prostitution occurs in several verses of the Qur'an. Two such references are given in the story of Mary and the birth of Prophet

4. The reference in this verse is to married slave women.

Jesus: 'She said: "How shall I have a child when no man has ever touched me and I have never been a loose woman?" (19: 20) 'At length, she went to her people carrying the child. They said: 'Mary, you have indeed done an amazing thing! Sister of Aaron, your father was not a wicked man, nor was your mother a loose woman!' (19: 27-28)

'Do not force your maids to prostitution when they desire to preserve their chastity, in order to make some worldly gain. If anyone should force them, then after they have been compelled, God will be much-forgiving, ever-merciful.' (24: 33)

Another condemned behaviour is to hurl false accusations on chaste women. God says: 'As for those who accuse chaste women [of adultery], and cannot produce four witnesses, flog them with eighty stripes; and do not accept their testimony ever after; for they are indeed transgressors.' (24: 4)

'And as for those who accuse their own wives [of adultery], but have no witnesses except themselves, let each of them call God four times to witness that he is indeed telling the truth; and the fifth time, that God's curse be upon him if he is telling a lie. However, punishment is averted from her if she calls God four times to witness that he is indeed telling a lie; and the fifth time, that God's wrath be upon her if he is telling the truth.' (24: 6-9)

We remind our readers of what we quoted of Qur'anic verses referring to believers' enjoyment of sexual pleasure in their future lives in Heaven.

Five: Hadith texts with an element of sex education

There are several references in the Prophet's statements to the private parts or genitalia. Jābir mentions that the Prophet (peace be upon him) said: 'Fear God in your treatment of women. You have taken them to yourselves with God's trust and their private parts are lawful to you by God's word.' [Related by Muslim]

'Abdullāh ibn 'Umar mentions that the Prophet (peace be upon him) said to the married couple who exchanged curses under oath: 'You will be accountable to God, as one of you is a liar. [He said to the man]: You have no right to her.' The man said: 'My money.' The Prophet said: 'You get nothing. If you had told the truth in your accusation, the dowry is for her being your lawful wife,[5] and if you lied about her, it is even further from you.' [Related by al-Bukhari and Muslim]

Abu Hurayrah mentions that God's Messenger (peace be upon him) said: 'Whoever sets a slave free for God's sake, then for everyone of the slave's organs God frees an organ of his from the Fire, including one genital for the other.' [Related by Muslim]

'Abdullāh ibn 'Umar said: "Umar ibn al-Khaṭṭāb mentioned to God's Messenger (peace be upon him) that he may be in a state of ceremonial impurity at night. The Prophet said to him: 'Perform the ablution and wash your penis, then go to sleep.' [Related by al-Bukhari]

In the long hadith describing the Prophet's pilgrimage, Jābir mentions: 'The Prophet (peace be upon him) arrived [in Makkah] on the morning of the fourth of Dhul-Ḥijjah. When we arrived he ordered us to release ourselves from consecration... He was informed that we said: "Now that there are only five days before the Day of Arafat, he is telling us we may consort with our wives. Thus we will go to Arafat with our genitals dripping with semen!' [Related by al-Bukhari and Muslim]

A number of hadiths refer to the front and anal parts of men and women. Jābir mentions that "the Jews used to claim that if a man

5. A more literal translation is: 'for her genital being lawful for you to enjoy.'

has intercourse with his wife from the rear (in Muslim's version: If the woman is approached from behind in her vagina), the child will be cross-eyed. Then God revealed the verse that says: 'Your wives are your tilth; go, then, to your tilth as you may desire, but first provide something for your souls. Fear God and know that you shall meet Him. Give the happy news to the believers."' (2: 223) [Related by al-Bukhari and Muslim]

Abu Hurayrah narrated that God's Messenger (peace be upon him) said: 'The Last Hour shall not arrive until the buttocks of the Daws women will have swayed before Dhul-Khalaṣah.' [Related by al-Bukhari and Muslim] Dhul-Khalaṣah was the idol the Daws tribe worshipped in pre-Islamic days.

'Amr ibn Salamah narrated: 'No one had learnt of the Qur'an more than I... They put me forward [to lead the prayer] when I was only six or seven years of age. I was wearing a cloak which would shrink when I prostrated myself. A local woman said: "Will you not cover your reciter's behind for us."' [Related by al-Bukhari]

'Ā'ishah narrated that God's Messenger (peace be upon him) said: 'You shall be resurrected bare-footed, naked, uncircumcised.' I said: 'Messenger of God, does this apply to men and women: they look at each other?' He said: 'The situation is too hard to think of that.' [Related by al-Bukhari and Muslim]

Hadith texts referring to women's organs

Some hadiths mention a woman's breast: Abu Sa'īd al-Khudrī mentioned that the Prophet said: 'Their [i.e. the Khawārij] distinctive sign is that in their ranks there will be a black man, with one of his upper arms looking like a woman's breast, or a shaking piece.' [Related by al-Bukhari]

‘Abdullāh ibn ‘Amr said that a woman came and said: ‘Messenger of God, this son of mine: he grew in my tummy and fed from my breast. My lap was his caring place. His father has divorced me and now he wants to take him away from me.’ The Prophet said to her: ‘You are more entitled to him unless you get married.’ [Related by Abu Dāwūd]

Other hadiths refer to a woman’s thigh: ‘Ā’ishah, the Prophet’s wife narrated: ‘Abu Bakr came over to me while God’s Messenger had placed his head on my thigh and slept. He said: “You have stopped God’s Messenger when the people are near no water spring and they have no water.” ‘Ā’ishah said: Abu Bakr remonstrated with me, and he poked me on my waist. Nothing stopped me from moving except the fact that God’s Messenger’s head was on my thigh.’ [Related by al-Bukhari and Muslim]

‘Ā’ishah reports: ‘God’s Messenger said when he was in good health: “Every Prophet was shown his place in heaven before he died, and then he was given a choice.” When the angels came to God’s Messenger (peace be upon him), his head was on my thigh. He was unconscious for a while, then he came to. He lifted his eyes to the ceiling and said: “My Lord, to the Highest Companion.”’ [Related by al-Bukhari and Muslim]

Women’s chests and necks are also mentioned in hadiths: ‘Ā’ishah narrated: ‘‘Abd al-Raḥmān ibn Abu Bakr entered to see the Prophet, as I was supporting him on my chest... He then passed away.’ In a different version: ‘He passed away in my home on the day of my turn, and I was holding him between my chest and neck.’ [Related by al-Bukhari].

Abu Burdah ibn Abu Mūsā al-Ash‘arī reports: ‘Abu Mūsā was ill, and he lost consciousness while his head was on the lap of a woman from his family.’ [Related by al-Bukhari]

Another part of a woman's body mentioned in a hadith is her cheek. 'Ā'ishah reports: 'It was the Day of Eid, and the Africans played with leather shields and spears. Either I asked the Prophet, or he said to me: "Do you like to watch?" I said: "Yes." He put me behind him, with my cheek on his cheek. He said to them: "Carry on, People of Arfidah." When I had enough, he asked me: "Have you had enough?" I said: "Yes." He then said: "You may go."' [Related by al-Bukhari and Muslim]

Some hadith texts refer to intercourse between man and wife. Judāmah bint Wahb said: 'I attended God's Messenger when he was with some people. He said: "I wanted to prohibit intercourse during the time of breastfeeding, but I noted that the Byzantines and the Persians practise this and it does not harm their children in any way."' [Related by Muslim]

A clear reference to sexual intercourse occurs in the story of the three Companions of the Prophet who did not join him on the Expedition of Tabuk. In his full account of their case, Ka'b ibn Mālik said: 'When we had spent 40 nights in that situation, with no revelation being given, a messenger from the Prophet came to me and said: "God's Messenger (peace be upon him) commands you to stay away from your wife." I asked whether that meant that I should divorce her or what should I do? He answered: No, but stay away from her. My two companions also received the same instructions. I told my wife to go to her people and stay with them until God would give his judgement in this matter. Hilāl ibn Umayyah's wife went to the Prophet and said: "Messenger of God, Hilāl ibn Umayyah is very old and has no servant. Do you mind if I continue to look after him?" He said: "That is all right, but do not let him come near you." She said: "By God, these things are far from his mind. He has not stopped crying ever since this has happened to him."' [Related by al-Bukhari and Muslim]

Hadith texts encouraging intercourse and full pleasure

Jābir mentions: 'We, the Prophet's Companions, started with the declared intention of performing the hajj only, without the 'umrah... The Prophet (peace be upon him) arrived [in Makkah] in the morning of the fourth of Dhul-Ḥijjah. When we arrived he ordered us to release ourselves from consecration... He was informed that we said: "Now that there are only five days before the Day of Arafat, he is telling us we may consort with our wives. Thus we will go to Arafat with our genitals dripping with semen!'... The Prophet addressed us and said: "You know that I am the most God-fearing among you and the most truthful, seeking what is good for you. Had it not been for that I brought my sacrifice with me, I would have released myself from consecration, as you do. Do it now. Were I to start afresh, I would not bring my sacrifice with me."' We, therefore, released ourselves from consecration in full obedience.' [Related by al-Bukhari and Muslim]

Jābir reported that he said to God's Messenger (peace be upon him): 'I got married recently.' He asked: 'Have you married a virgin or a mature woman?' I said: 'She is a mature woman.' He said: 'Would it not have been better for you to marry a young one: you would play with her and she would play with you; and you have fun together?' (In another version: 'So that you make her laugh and she makes you laugh.' And in a third version: 'You miss out on a virgin and her watering mouth.') [Related by al-Bukhari and Muslim]

'Alqamah narrated: 'I was with 'Abdullāh when 'Uthmān met him at Mina. He said: 'Abu 'Abd al-Raḥmān, I have a word to say to you. They talked together, and 'Uthmān said to him: 'Abu 'Abd al-Raḥmān, would you like us to get you a virgin wife so that she would remind you of what you used to have?' When 'Abdullāh showed that he had no interest in this, he pointed to me and said: 'O 'Alqamah.' I paid attention to him as he said: 'Since you say that, the Prophet (peace be upon him) said to us: "Young people, whoever of you can afford marriage, should get married."' [Related by al-Bukhari and Muslim]

Seeking a ruling on intercourse:

Ubay ibn Ka'b said that he asked God's Messenger (peace be upon him): 'If a man had intercourse with his wife but did not ejaculate [what is required]?' (In a different version by Muslim: 'A man is intimate with his wife but then slackens.') The Prophet said: 'He washes the part that touched the woman, then performs the ablution and offers his prayers.' [Related by al-Bukhari and Muslim]

Zayd ibn Khālid mentioned... that he asked 'Uthmān ibn 'Affān: 'Suppose a man has intercourse but did not discharge?' 'Uthmān said: 'He performs the ablution as he normally does for prayer, after washing his penis.' [Related by al-Bukhari and Muslim]

Abu Sa'īd al-Khudrī said that 'Itbān asked: 'Messenger of God, suppose a man withdraws from his wife, without having ejaculated. What should he do?' The Prophet: 'A bath only becomes due if ejaculation occurs.'[6] [Related by Muslim]

Women ask men for rulings on matters related to sex

Asmā' narrated: 'A woman came to the Prophet and said: "A woman may drop some menses on her clothes: what should she do?" He said: "She should rub it off, then rub it with her wet hand. She then sprinkles water on it, then she can wear it when she prays."' [Related by al-Bukhari and Muslim]

'Ā'ishah narrated: 'Fāṭimah bint Abi Ḥubaysh came to the Prophet and said: "Messenger of God, I am a woman who continues in menstruation without an end. Am I to leave off prayer?" The Prophet said: "No. This is [haemorrhage from] a blood vessel, not menstruation. When your

---

6. The ruling in this hadith and the two before it is abrogated and replaced by the subsequent hadith in which the Prophet says: 'When the two genitals have met, a bath becomes obligatory.' – Author's note.

period comes, stop praying, and when it is over, wash the blood off yourself and resume praying... Then perform the ablution for every prayer when it is time for it.' [Related by al-Bukhari and Muslim]

'Ā'ishah, the Prophet's wife, narrated: 'Umm Ḥabībah bint Jaḥsh (God's Messenger's sister-in-law and 'Abd al-Raḥmān ibn 'Awf's wife) continued to have a discharge for seven years. She asked God's Messenger about this. He said: "This is not menstruation, but haemorrhage from a blood vessel. Wash yourself and pray." 'Ā'ishah said: 'She used to perform the *ghusl* using a tub in Zaynab's, her sister's, compartment, and the water would become red because of the blood.' [Related by Muslim]

Anas ibn Mālik narrated: 'Umm Sulaym (who was Isḥāq's grandmother) came to God's Messenger (peace be upon him) as 'Ā'ishah was with him. She said: "Messenger of God, [may I ask about] a woman who sees in her dream what a man sees, seeing of herself what a man sees of himself?" 'Ā'ishah said: "Umm Sulaym, you have shamed women! How shameful!" The Prophet said to 'Ā'ishah: "Rather shame to you! Yes, Umm Sulaym. She must take a bath if she sees that."' [Related by Muslim]

Subay'ah bint al-Ḥārith, a companion of the Prophet, reports that she was married to Sa'd ibn Khawlah, a Companion of the Prophet who took part in the Battle of Badr... He died during the Prophet's pilgrimage. Only a short while after that she gave birth to her child. When she regained her strength, she started to wear make-up expecting a proposal. (In the version related by Ahmad: she wore kohl, henna and put on a good appearance.) Abu al-San'bil ibn Ba'kak came to her and said: "How come you are adorned expecting a proposal, hoping to get married? By God, you cannot get married before the lapse of four months and ten days [after your husband's death]." Subay'ah said: 'When he said this to me, I put on my clothes in the evening and went to God's Messenger (peace be upon him) and

I asked him about this. He told me that I have finished my waiting period when I gave birth and he left it up to me to get married if I wished.' [Related by al-Bukhari and Muslim]

Men ask women for rulings on matters related to sex

Abu Bakr ibn 'Abd al-Raḥmān ibn al-Ḥārith said: 'I heard Abu Hurayrah say in his narrations: "Whoever happens to be in a state of ceremonial impurity when the Fajr Prayer becomes due may not fast." I mentioned this to 'Abd al-Raḥmān ibn al-Ḥārith and he disagreed. 'Abd al-Raḥmān then set out and I accompanied him. We went to 'Ā'ishah and Umm Salamah. 'Abd al-Raḥmān asked them about this and both said: "The Prophet (peace be upon him) would in the morning be in a state of ceremonial impurity, but not through a wet dream, and he would fast."' [Related by al-Bukhari and Muslim]

Sulaymān ibn Yasār reported that he asked Umm Salamah whether a man may fast if he finds himself in the morning in a state of ceremonial impurity. She said: 'God's Messenger (peace be upon him) would in the morning be in a state of ceremonial impurity, not through a wet dream, and he would fast.' [Related by Muslim]

We note that the women, who were Companions of the Prophet, did not start by putting their questions to the Prophet's wives. They asked him directly. Nor did the Prophet (peace be upon him) draw the women's attention to ask his wives first. Likewise, the men who belonged to the *tābi'īn* generation did not send their women to 'Ā'ishah, requesting information. The men went to her directly. This makes it clear that there is nothing wrong in seeking religious information about sexual matters from the highest authority, even when such authority belongs to the opposite sex.

This was the normal practice. Indeed one of the Prophet's Companions sent his wife twice to ask the Prophet about a certain matter related to sex. 'Aṭā' ibn Yasār narrated that an Anṣārī man kissed his wife when he was fasting. He told his wife to go and ask the Prophet about this. She went and asked him. The Prophet said to her: 'I do that.' Her husband said to her: 'God may give His Messenger any concession He wishes.' She went back to the Prophet [and told him]. He said: 'I am the one who knows best the limits set by God and I am the most God-fearing'. [Related by 'Abd al-Razzāq]

We also find among the Prophet's Companions a woman complaining to her father-in-law about something of the private matters between a married couple. 'Abdullāh ibn 'Amr narrated: 'My father married me to a woman of good family. He used to enquire after his daughter-in-law and ask her about her husband. She said: 'He is a fine man who has never been with us in bed and never lifted a cover of ours ever since we have been together.' [Related by al-Bukhari]

Indeed, a woman mentions something of the private matters between a married couple to her husband's friend, both of whom were Companions of the Prophet (peace be upon him): Abu Juḥayfah narrated: 'The Prophet established a bond of brotherhood between Salmān and Abu al-Dardā.' Once Salmān went to visit Abu al-Dardā' and saw his wife wearing plain clothes. He asked her the reason and she told him: "Your brother, Abu al-Dardā', does not care for anything in this life."' [Related by al-Bukhari]

Some incidents from the Prophet's time show that there was no embarrassment if people saw some indications of what a man does with his wife. Abu Hurayrah narrated: 'The prayer was announced and the congregation stood in their rows. God's Messenger (peace be upon him) then came over and stood at his place, but he then remembered that he was in a state of ceremonial impurity. He said to us: 'Stay in your place. He went back, took a [quick] bath and came back to us, with his head dripping with water. He started the prayer and we prayed with him.' [Related by al-Bukhari and Muslim]

Sulaymān ibn Yasār said: 'I asked 'Ā'ishah about semen falling on one's clothes.' She said: 'I used to wash it off the Prophet's robe and he would go out to prayer, with the effect of the washing clearly apparent as wet spots.' [Related by al-Bukhari and Muslim]

Sometimes the effects of being together with one's bride were clearly visible. Anas narrated that the Prophet noticed traces of saffron on 'Abd al-Raḥmān ibn 'Awf. He asked him about it. He said: "I have married an Anṣārī woman giving a dowry equal to the weight of a date stone in gold." The Prophet said: "May God make it a blessing for you."' [Related by al-Bukhari and Muslim]

We even note that one of the Prophet's wives encouraged her nephew to kiss his wife in her presence. Abu al-Naḍr mentions that 'Ā'ishah bint Ṭalḥah[7] was with 'Ā'ishah [the Prophet's wife] when her own husband ['Abdullāh] ibn 'Abd al-Raḥmān ibn Abu Bakr arrived. 'Ā'ishah said to him: 'What stops you from coming close to your wife, speaking to her and kissing her?' He said: 'Would I kiss her when I am fasting?' She said: 'Yes.' [Related by Mālik in *al-Muwaṭṭa*.']

Taking care to provide the clearest explanation

It was characteristic of the first Muslim generation that knowledge about Islam should be clearly stated, with nothing suppressed, even if a person had to overcome shyness. 'Ā'ishah narrated: 'God's Messenger (peace be upon him) used to kiss anyone of his wives when he was fasting. She then smiled.' Her smile might have been an expression of disapproval of the opposite view. Others said that she smiled wondering at herself saying this when women normally are too shy to speak about it to men. Yet she was obliged to speak

7. 'Ā'ishah bint Ṭalḥah was 'Ā'ishah's niece. Her mother was Umm Kulthūm bint Abu Bakr. Her father was Ṭalḥah ibn 'Ubaydullāh, one of the earliest Companions of the Prophet.

about it, so that knowledge would not be suppressed. On the other hand, her smile was an expression of modesty, as she was speaking of herself, or to alert the listener to the fact that it was her case, and as such, it was most reliable.

The Prophet himself was very keen to give very clear explanations. 'Umar ibn Abu Salamah, the Prophet's stepson, reports that he asked God's Messenger (peace be upon him): 'May a fasting person kiss [his wife]?' The Prophet said: 'Ask this one,' pointing to Umm Salamah [who was 'Umar's mother]. She told him that God's Messenger did that. He said: 'Messenger of God, God has forgiven you your past and future sins.' The Prophet said to him: 'By God, I am the one among you who fears God most.' [Related by Muslim]

'Ā'ishah, the Prophet's wife, said that a man asked God's Messenger (peace be upon him) about the case of a man who has intercourse with his wife, then he slackens: are they required to have a bath? 'Ā'ishah was present. The Prophet (peace be upon him) said to him: 'I do the same with this one, then we take a bath.' [Related by Muslim]

The Prophet's wives, Mothers of the Believers, were always ready and keen to give clear explanations. Abu Bakr ibn 'Abd al-Raḥmān narrated: 'I was with my father and I went with him and visited 'Ā'ishah (may God be pleased with her). She said: "I bear witness that God's Messenger (peace be upon him) would in the morning be in a state of ceremonial impurity, through intercourse, not a wet dream, then remain fasting that day.' We then visited Umm Salamah and she said the same thing.' [Related by al-Bukhari and Muslim]

Zaynab bint Abi Salamah narrated that [her mother] Umm Salamah said: 'I was with the Prophet under a velvet cover when I started my period. I dropped off quietly, picked up my menstruation gear and put it on. God's Messenger (peace be upon him) said to me: "Are you having your period?" I said that I was. He told me to come in and brought me close to him under the cover.' [Zaynab] said: 'She also told me that the Prophet used to kiss her when he was fasting. She said: "I used to take a bath with the Prophet taking water from the same container, to remove our state of ceremonial impurity."' [Related by al-Bukhari and Muslim]

'Urwah ibn al-Zubayr narrated that 'Ā'ishah said: 'God's Messenger (peace be upon him) used to kiss anyone of his wives when he was fasting. She then smiled.' In Muslim's version: al-Qāsim ibn Muhammad ibn Abu Bakr narrated that 'Ā'ishah said: 'The Prophet used to kiss his wives when he was fasting.' [Related by al-Bukhari and Muslim]

'Abdullāh ibn Shihāb al-Khawlānī said: 'I was staying at 'Ā'ishah's when I had a wet dream. As I was wearing my two garments [at the time], I soaked them in water. 'Ā'ishah's maid saw me and informed her. 'Ā'ishah sent to me asking: "Why did you do this with your two garments?" I said: I saw what a sleeping person may see in his dream. She said: "Did you see anything on them?" I said: No. She said: "If you see something, you wash it. I can see myself as I rubbed it off God's Messenger's robe, with my nail, when it was dry."' [Related by Muslim]

The Prophet's Companions were also very keen to state Islamic rulings very clearly. Jābir reports that God's Messenger (peace be upon him) saw a woman, and he went to his wife Zaynab as she was dying a piece of leather. He had with her whatever he wanted. He then came out and said to his Companions: 'A woman comes in the form of a devil and goes away in the form of a devil[8]. If any of you sees a woman, he should go to his wife. That will clear what he experiences.' [Related by Muslim]

8. This expression refers to the natural feeling of temptation when a man sees a woman. - Author's note.

Muʿāwiyah ibn Abi Sufyān narrated that he asked his sister, Umm Ḥabībah, the Prophet's wife: 'Did God's Messenger pray wearing the same garment he was wearing when he had intercourse with her?' She said: 'Yes, he did if he saw nothing on it.' [Related by Abu Dāwūd]

Dhafīf narrated: 'Ibn ʿAbbās was asked about coitus interruptus. He called in a slave woman of his and said to her: 'Tell them.' She seemed too shy. He said: 'It is such. As for me, I do it', meaning that he resorted to it.' [Related by Mālik in *al-Muwaṭṭa*.']

Special cases related to intimacy between husband and wife

Anas ibn Mālik reports: 'One of Abu Ṭalḥah's children by Umm Sulaym died. She said to her family: "Please do not say anything to Abu Ṭalḥah about his son until I have broken the news to him." When her husband came in, she gave him a good dinner. Then after the meal, she put on her best appearance, and he made love to her. When she realized that he was fully satisfied, she said to him: "Abu Ṭalḥah! If some people lend something to their neighbours, and then they requested their article back, can the others refuse?" He said: "No." She said: "Then, seek God's reward for the loss of your son..." He was angry, and said to her: "You kept me unaware until I have stained myself, then told me about my son." He then went to the Prophet and told him. The Prophet said to him: "May God bless you both for what you did last night." Anas said: "Umm Sulaym was subsequently pregnant and she gave birth to a son."' [Related by al-Bukhari and Muslim. This is Muslim's version]

We note that the narrator is keen to report the details that people normally feel too diffident to mention. He gives these details in order to highlight Umm Sulaym's [who was his own mother] merit, resigned acceptance of God's will and total trust in Him. Muslim women will do well to follow the example of such a distinguished Companion of the Prophet.

ʿIkrimah narrated that Rifāʿah divorced his wife, and she got married to ʿAbd al-Raḥmān ibn al-Zabīr al-Quraẓī. ʿĀ'ishah said: 'She was wearing a green head cover. She put her complaint to her and showed her that her skin was getting green. When the Prophet came in – and women stand by women – ʿĀ'ishah said: "I have not seen anything like what women suffer. Her skin was darker than her garment."'

Her husband was informed that she went to see God's Messenger (peace be upon him). He came over with his two sons by another wife. She said: "By God, I have done him no wrong. But what he has does not give me more than this (picking the tip of her dress). (In another version: He did not touch me except once when he gave me nothing). (Yet in a different version: Khālid ibn Saʿīd was standing at the door as he was not given permission to enter. He heard what she said. Therefore, he said: "Abu Bakr, will you not stop this woman saying this openly at God's Messenger's place?" By God, the Prophet did no more than smile). Her husband said: "She lies, Messenger of God. I go into her like an eager man, but she is rebellious and wants to go back to Rifāʿah." The Prophet said: "If so, you shall not be lawful to him until he has experienced your sweetness." The Prophet saw his two sons who were with him. He asked: "Are these your sons?" He said: "Yes." The Prophet said to her: "And you claim what you do about him? By God, they are more similar to him than one crow is similar to another."' [Related by al-Bukhari and Muslim]

Salamah ibn Ṣakhr al-Anṣārī narrated: 'As a man, I could have sexual intercourse as other men could not. When Ramadan started, I separated myself from my wife, making her forbidden to me until Ramadan would be over, fearing to consort with her at night and then continue non-stop until the morning. One night, when she was serving me, a part of her body was exposed to me, and I jumped on her. In the morning, I went to my people and told them of what happened. I also said: "Come with me to see God's Messenger (peace be upon him) and I tell him what happened." They said: "No. By

God, we shall not do that. We fear that Qur'anic revelations might be given about us, or that God's Messenger may say to us something and we will be shamed with it forever. It is better that you go alone and do what you need to do." I left them and went to God's Messenger and told him my story. He said: "And you did that?" I said: I did that. He said: "And you did that?" I said: I did that. He said: "And you did that?" I said: I did that. Here I am. Apply to me God's verdict, and I will bear it with patience. He said: "Free a slave."[9] I slapped myself on my neck and said: By Him who has sent you with the message of the truth, I own none but this. He said: "Then fast for two months." I said: Messenger of God, has this trouble befallen me through anything other than fasting? He said: "Then feed sixty needy people." I said: By Him who sent you with the message of the truth, we spent last night hungry, having no dinner. He said: "Then go to the man in charge of the zakat of the Zurayq clan and tell him to give it to you. Give one *wasq* of food to sixty needy people on your own behalf and use the rest for yourself and your family." I went back to my people and said: You only gave me strictness and wrong opinion, but with God's Messenger (peace be upon him) I found ease and blessing. He has ordered that you give me your zakat. I may now have it. So they paid it to me.' [Related by al-Tirmidhī]

Ibn 'Abbās narrated that 'A man came to the Prophet telling him that he had stated the oath making his wife forbidden to him, then had intercourse with her. He said: "Messenger of God, I had forbidden myself my wife, then had intercourse with her before making the atonement." The Prophet said: "What caused you to do so, may God have mercy on you?" The man said: "I saw her anklet in the moon light." The Prophet said: "Do not come near her until you have done what God has commanded you to do."' [Related by al-Tirmidhī]

9. The normal expression used at the time for 'free a slave' is literally translated as 'set one neck free.' This explains the narrator's gesture in response.

Abu Saʿīd al-Khudrī narrated that God's Messenger (peace be upon him) sent a message to an Anṣārī man. He came with his head dripping with water. The Prophet said to him: 'Perhaps we have hastened you.' The man said: 'Yes.' The Prophet said: 'If you are hastened, or if you have intercourse without ejaculation, you only need to perform the ablution.'[10] (In Muslim's version: The man came, dragging his lower garment. God's Messenger said: We have hastened the man.) [Related by al-Bukhari and Muslim]

ʿIkrimah narrated: "ʿAbdullāh ibn Rawāḥah was reclining next to his wife. He then went up to his slave woman.' He narrated that his wife saw him on top of the slave woman and he denied it. She asked him to recite the Qur'an, knowing that a person in a state of ceremonial impurity does not recite the Qur'an. Instead, he recited these lines of poetry:

> Among us is God's Messenger reciting His Book, when the light of dawn spreads.
> He has shown us guidance after we had been blind. Now our hearts believe that what he says is certain to happen.
> He drags himself out of bed for night worship while the unbelievers remain asleep.
> She said: "I believe in God and belie my eyesight." He related this to the Prophet who smiled broadly, with his teeth becoming visible.'

Asmā' bint Abu Bakr narrated: 'We set out in *iḥrām*. God's Messenger (peace be upon him) said: "Whoever has brought his sacrifice stays in *iḥrām*, and those who have not brought a sacrifice release themselves from *iḥrām*." I did not have a sacrifice and therefore I released myself,

10. This ruling that only the normal ablution is needed in such a case was subsequently abrogated by the hadith: 'If the two genitals meet, a bath becomes obligatory.'

but al-Zubayr[11] brought his sacrifice with him and he did not release himself.' She said: 'I put on my clothes and came out and sat with al-Zubayr. He said: "Leave me alone." I said: Do you fear that I will jump on you?' [Related by Muslim]

Rabī'ah ibn Abi 'Abd al-Raḥmān narrated that a man went to al-Qāsim ibn Muhammad and said: 'After attending at Arafat I proceeded to Mina with my wife. Then I moved away into a mountain corner. As I came close to my wife, she said: "I have not shortened my hair yet."[12] I cut some of her hair with my teeth, then I had intercourse with her.' Al-Qāsim smiled and said to him: 'Tell her to cut a bit of her hair with scissors.' [Related by Mālik in *al-Muwaṭṭa.*']

11. Al-Zubayr was her husband.
12. This means that she had not yet released herself from consecration. As such, intercourse was still forbidden for her. Hence, her husband cut her hair with his teeth.

CHAPTER III

Acknowledgement of the Strength of Sexual Desire

- The strong temptation of sex
- Strong but must be faced
- A strong urge and falling into sin

Acknowledgement of the Strength of Sexual Desire

The strong temptation of sex

Humans are God's creation and He knows best what He has planted of temptation in their nature. He says: 'How could it be that He who has created should not know all? He is above all comprehension, yet is all-aware.' (67: 14) One of the strongest human desires is love of the other sex, which essentially means sexual desire. Various texts from the Qur'an and the Sunnah confirm its strength, including: 'Alluring to man is the enjoyment of worldly desires through women and offspring, heaped-up treasures of gold and silver, horses of high mark, cattle and plantations. These are the comforts of this life. With God is the best of all goals.' (3: 14)

God says: 'God wants to lighten your burdens; for man has been created weak.' (4: 28) This verse confirms man's weakness and that man finds the sexual urge difficult to control. In his commentary on the Qur'an, al-Ṭabarī quotes 'Ikrimah and Mujāhid saying that the reference in this verse to man's being weak means that men are strongly attracted to women.

Because of this weakness and the need to provide lawful ways of satisfying sexual desire to all believers, Islam made it permissible for Muslim men to marry slave women, when slavery was a universal social institution. This was in the case of a believer who was poor and did not have the means to marry a free woman. God says: 'Any of you who, owing to circumstances, is not in a position to marry a free believing woman may marry a believing maiden from among those whom your right hands possess. God knows all about your faith: you belong to one another.' (4: 25) Yet this is a concession that is tied to a condition, which is clearly stated in the same verse: 'This provision applies to those of you who fear to stumble into sin.' This means that this concession is granted by God to His servants who are of limited means, so that they are protected from falling into sin.

Usāmah ibn Zayd narrated that the Prophet (peace be upon him) said: 'I do not leave behind a worse temptation for men than women.' [Related by al-Bukhari and Muslim]. Abu Sa'īd al-Khudrī quotes the Prophet (peace be upon him) saying: 'Beware of [the temptation of] women. The first deviation by the Children of Israel was through [the temptation of] women.' [Related by Muslim]

Strong but must be faced

Many of the early Companions of the Prophet were young men, and the hard times that Islam was facing did not enable many of them to get married. They had to struggle against their strong sexual urges. Sa'd ibn Abi Waqqāṣ reports: 'God's Messenger (peace be upon him) rejected 'Uthmān ibn Maẓ'ūn's wish to remain celibate. Had he permitted him, we would have emasculated ourselves.' [Related by al-Bukhari and Muslim] A different version related by al-Ṭabarānī is as follows: '‘Uthmān ibn Maẓ‘ūn said: "Messenger of God, I find celibacy too hard. Permit me to emasculate myself." The Prophet said: "No. Resort to fasting instead."'

‘Abdullāh ibn Mas‘ūd reported: 'We used to go on jihad with God's Messenger (peace be upon him), and we had nothing. [In Muslim's version: we had no women] We thought of emasculating ourselves, but God's Messenger forbade us.' [Related by al-Bukhari and Muslim]

In the face of this strong urge, the proper way to stick to the virtuous course is early marriage, which the Prophet encouraged. ‘Abdullāh ibn Mas‘ūd narrated: 'We were young men with the Prophet and had nothing. God's Messenger said to us: "Young men, whoever of you can afford it, should get married. It helps to lower one's gaze and maintain chastity. Whoever cannot afford it should resort to fasting, as it reduces desire.' [Related by al-Bukhari and Muslim] Al-Mustawrid ibn Shaddād said: 'I heard the Prophet (peace be upon him) say: "Whoever is undertaking an assignment for us [i.e. for the Muslim state] should have a wife."' [Related by Abu Dāwūd]

It is natural, considering the strong sexual urge, that when a married man is away from home, he looks forward to be reunited with his wife. Abu Hurayrah narrated that the Prophet (peace be upon him) said: 'An earlier prophet went on a military expedition. He said to his people: "Whoever has contracted a marriage with a woman and wants to consummate the marriage but has not yet done so should not join me [on this expedition].' [Related by al-Bukhari]

Jābir narrated: 'I was with God's Messenger on an expedition. When we were on the way back, I tried to speed, riding a slow camel, when another rider caught up with me. I turned back and found that he was God's Messenger (peace be upon him). He said: "Why are you in haste?" I said: I only recently got married.' (In another version: I said: Messenger of God, I am a recent husband. I asked his permission and he granted it. I went ahead of other people to Madinah) [Related by al-Bukhari and Muslim]

Abu Sa'īd narrated: 'A woman came to the Prophet when we were with him. She said: "Messenger of God, my husband, Ṣafwān ibn al-Mu'aṭṭal, makes me break my fast when I voluntarily fast"... Ṣafwān said: "Messenger of God, as for her saying that I make her break her fast, she frequently fasts. I am a young man and I cannot resist [the urge]." God's Messenger said on that day: "No woman should fast voluntarily without her husband's permission." [Related by Abu Dāwūd]

The proper way to resist temptation is through marriage, or fasting if one is unable to get married. Jābir ibn 'Abdullāh said that God's Messenger (peace be upon him) said: 'If any of you sees a woman and is attracted by her, he should go to his wife and have intercourse with her. That is enough to remove what he has experienced.' [Related by Muslim]

'Abdullāh ibn Mas'ūd said: God's Messenger (peace be upon him) said to us: 'Young men, whoever of you is able to undertake the requirements of marriage should do so... Whoever is unable may resort to fasting, as it weakens desire.' [Related by al-Bukhari and Muslim]

A strong urge and falling into sin

Falling in sin means doing what is forbidden. In this area, different things are forbidden. Islam states a form of punishment for each type. We will discuss each type in some details.

Type 1: Intercourse with one's wife when it is not permissible

I. During the night in Ramadan (before removing the prohibition)

At the beginning, Muslims were not allowed to have intercourse with their wives during the nights of Ramadan. This restriction was subsequently removed, as God says: 'It is lawful for you to be intimate with your wives during the night preceding the fast. They are as a garment for you, as you are for them. God is aware that you have been deceiving yourselves in this respect, and He has turned to you in His mercy and pardoned you.' (2: 187)

Al-Barā' said: 'When the order to fast in the month of Ramadan was first given, men did not go near women for the whole month. However, some people were guilty of deceiving themselves. Therefore, God revealed: 'God is aware that you have been deceiving yourselves in this respect, and He has turned to you in His mercy and pardoned you.' [Related by al-Bukhari]

II. During the day of fasting

Abu Hurayrah reports: 'As we were sitting with God's Messenger (peace be upon him) a man came to him and said: "Messenger of God, I am ruined." (In another version the man said that he was burnt.) The Prophet said: "What happened to you?" He said: "I had intercourse with my wife when I was fasting." God's Messenger asked him: "Do you have a slave to set free?" He said: "No." The Prophet asked him: "Can you fast two consecutive months?" The man said: "No." The Prophet said: "Do you have the money to feed sixty poor people?" The man said: "No." The Prophet remained silent. As we were still sitting, the Prophet was brought a large sack full of dates. He said: "Where is the man who asked me?" (In another version: Where is the burnt man?) The man identified himself and the Prophet said: "Take this and give it away as charity?" The man said: "To anyone poorer than me, Messenger of God? By God, between these two sides of Madinah, no family is poorer than my family." The Prophet smiled widely, showing his teeth, then said to him: "Feed your family with this."' [Related by al-Bukhari and Muslim]

III. Intercourse after zihar [i.e. making one's wife prohibited to oneself]

Abu Salamah and Muhammad ibn ʿAbd al-Raḥmān narrated that Salmān ibn Ṣakhr al-Anṣārī, who belonged to the Bayāḍah clan, told his wife that she was to him like his mother's back until Ramadan was over. When half of Ramadan was over, he had intercourse with her during the night. He came to God's Messenger (peace be upon him) and told him. The Prophet told him: "Set a slave free." The man said: "I cannot afford it." The Prophet said: "Then fast two consecutive months." The man said: "I cannot do that." The Prophet said: "Then feed sixty poor people." He said: "I do not have the means." The Prophet said to Farwah ibn ʿAmr: "Give him that sack to feed sixty poor people." [Related by al-Tirmidhī] The sack mentioned in this hadith was a large one, holding fifteen or sixteen *ṣāʿ*, and a *ṣāʿ* is a measure estimated to be equal to 2.2 kilograms.

IV. Intercourse during consecration

Mālik said that he learnt that ʿUmar ibn al-Khaṭṭāb, ʿAlī ibn Abi Ṭālib and Abu Hurayrah were asked about a man who had intercourse with his wife when he was in a state of consecration, i.e. *iḥrām*. They said that both should continue their pilgrimage, then they had to perform the hajj again the following year and offer the sacrifice. ʿAlī ibn Abi Ṭālib added: 'When they start their hajj the following year, they stay away from each other until they finish their hajj.' [Related by Mālik]

Ibn ʿAbbās was asked about a man who had intercourse with his wife when he was at Mina and before performing the *ṭawāf* of *ifāḍah*. He ordered him to sacrifice a camel. [Related by Mālik]

Type 2: Committing minor sins

ʿAbdullāh ibn ʿUmar quotes the Prophet as saying: "Three people were out walking when it started to rain heavily. They went into a cave for shelter. However, they were trapped by a large rock. One of them suggested that they should pray to God [for their release] mentioning their best past actions. One of them said... Another said: 'My Lord! You know that I used to love a cousin of mine most passionately. (The version related by Muslim adds here the following: 'I tried to get to her but she repeatedly refused me, until one year there was a famine, and she came to me.) She said that I could not have her unless I paid her one hundred dīnārs. I tried hard until I raised the money. When I sat between her legs, she said to me: "Fear God and do not take me except lawfully." I rose and left her alone. My Lord! If you know that I only did that for Your sake, then remove this trap.' God removed two-thirds of their trap...." [Related by al-Bukhari and Muslim]

Ibn Masʿūd narrated that 'A man kissed a woman...' (In a different version: 'A man kissed or handled a woman....') (Yet another version mentions that the man said: 'I flirted with a woman in the far end of Madinah but did not have intercourse with her.') He went to the Prophet (peace be upon him) and told him. God revealed the verse that says: "Attend to your prayers at both ends of the day and in the early watches of the night. Surely, good deeds erase evil ones." (11: 114) The man said: 'Messenger of God, does this apply to me?' He said: 'It applies to all my community.' [Related by al-Bukhari and Muslim]

Anas narrated: 'A man came to the Prophet and said: "Messenger of God, I have committed a punishable offence. Enforce it on me."

The prayer was then called and he joined the congregational prayer led by God's Messenger (peace be upon him). When the prayer was over, he said: "Messenger of God, I have committed a punishable offence. Enforce it on me." The Prophet said: "Did you offer the prayer with us?" The man said: "Yes." The Prophet said: "You have been forgiven."' [Related by Muslim]

Type 3: Committing adultery

Buraydah narrated that Māʿiz ibn Mālik al-Aslamī came to the Prophet and said: 'Messenger of God, I have wronged myself by committing adultery. I would like you to purify me.' The Prophet turned him away. He came the following day and said: 'Messenger of God, I have committed adultery.' The Prophet again turned him away. The Prophet also sent to his people asking them: 'Do you know of anything wrong with his mind? Do you find anything odd about him?' They answered that they knew him as one of sound mind, and that he was devout. Māʿiz came to the Prophet a third time, and the Prophet sent them a similar message. They responded that they knew of nothing wrong with him or his mind. When he came a fourth time, the Prophet gave instructions and a hole was dug for him and he was stoned.

'The Ghāmidī woman came and said to the Prophet: "Messenger of God! I have committed adultery. Please arrange for my absolution through punishment." He sent her home. On the following day she came again and said: "Messenger of God! Why have you turned me back home! It may be that you wish to send me home like you did with Māʿiz. By God, I am pregnant." The Prophet said: "Now, you may not be punished. Go away and wait until you have given birth." When she was delivered of a boy, she brought him to the Prophet wrapped in a piece of cloth, and said: "I have given birth to this boy.' The Prophet said to her: 'Go away and breast-feed your baby until you have weaned him." She went away and waited until she had weaned the child, then brought him to the Prophet holding a piece of bread in his hand. She said: "Prophet! I have already weaned him and he is now eating ordinary food." The Prophet gave the child to a Muslim man. He then ordered a hole to be dug in the ground up to her chest. He told people to stone her to death.[13] Khālid ibn al-Walīd hit her with a stone on her head, and her blood splashed on his face; so he cursed her. When the Prophet heard him cursing her, he said to him: "Khālid, be calm. By Him who holds my soul in His hand, her repentance is so genuine that if one who levied tribute-money unjustly had similarly repented he would be pardoned." He then ordered that she should be prepared for burial and he offered the funeral prayer for her before she was buried.' [Related by Muslim]

'Imrān ibn Ḥuṣayn reported that a woman from the Juhaynah tribe came to the Prophet and she was pregnant through adultery. She said: 'Prophet, I have committed an offence with a mandatory punishment. Enforce it on me.' The Prophet called in her guardian. He said to him: 'Treat her kindly. When she has given birth, bring her to me.' The guardian did that. The Prophet gave instructions. Her garments were tied up on her. He then gave orders. She was stoned and he offered the funeral prayer for her....' [Related by Muslim]

Abu Hurayrah and Zayd ibn Khālid al-Juhanī narrated: 'A man came to the Prophet and said to him: "I appeal to you by God to judge between us according to God's Book." His opponent, who was more learned, stood up and said: "He makes a fair request. Please judge between us according to God's Book, but let me speak first." The Prophet told him to say what he wanted. He said: "My son was

13. As this is the mandatory punishment when the crime of adultery is established through voluntary and repeated confession, it cannot be waived or reduced by any authority, not even the Prophet. Hence, the Prophet had no option but to implement it, even though the hadith shows that her repentance would have been sufficient, had she not voluntarily confessed to her crime.

working for this man and he committed adultery with his wife. I settled the case with him by giving him 100 sheep and a servant. I then asked some learned people and they told me that my son's punishment is 100 lashes and that he be sent into exile for a year, while this man's wife is to be stoned." The Prophet said: "By Him who holds my soul in His hand, I will judge between you two according to God's Book: the sheep and the servant are to be returned to you. Your son is to be whipped 100 lashes and sent into exile for a year. You, Unays, go to this man's wife and ask her. If she confesses her guilt, then stone her." She admitted her guilt and she was stoned.' [Related by al-Bukhari and Muslim]

Jābir ibn Samurah narrated: 'God's Messenger was brought a short muscular man with thick hair, wearing a lower garment. He had committed adultery. The Prophet turned him away twice, but then he ordered the enforcement of punishment. The man was then stoned. The Prophet said: "Will it be that whenever we set out to fight for God's cause that someone from among you strongly feels the sexual urge and commits adultery? If God hands any such person to me, I shall severely punish him.'

Wā'il al-Kindī reported that 'A woman was raped by a man as she was going to the mosque in the darkness at dawn. She appealed to a passer by for help but the rapist ran away. Then a group of people passed by her and she appealed to them for help. They caught up with the one to whom she had appealed but the other [i.e. the rapist] managed to run away. They brought her the man they caught. He said to her: I am the one who helped you, but the other has run away. They took him to God's Messenger (peace be upon him)....' [Related by Ahmad]

Ibn 'Abbās reported that Hilāl ibn Umayyah accused his wife of having committed adultery. He came forward and testified, (meaning that he called God four times to witness that he was indeed telling the truth; and the fifth time, that God's curse be upon him if he was telling a lie). The Prophet said to them that God knew that one of them was lying; but would either turn to God in repentance? His wife stood up and testified, (meaning that she called God four times to witness that he was indeed telling a lie; and the fifth time, that God's wrath be upon her if he was telling the truth). [Related by al-Bukhari and Muslim]

Abu Hurayrah and Zayd ibn Khālid narrated: 'God's Messenger (peace be upon him) was asked about a slave woman who is unmarried and commits fornication. He said: "If she commits sinful fornication punish her by flogging; then if she commits it again, flog her; then if again, flog her then sell her even for a paltry price.' [Related by al-Bukhari and Muslim]

CHAPTER IV

Islam Facilitates Lawful Ways of Enjoying Sexual Pleasure

- Aspects of facilitating sexual enjoyment

Islam Facilitates Lawful Ways of Enjoying Sexual Pleasure

Islam appreciates that humans have a strong sexual desire which they need to satisfy. As we mentioned earlier, Islam takes care to ensure that all things that help to facilitate human needs are provided, so that Muslims will not have to endure difficulty. They will thus be able to live their lives enjoying physical and mental health. Thus, Islam gives clear evidence of God's mercy which He bestows on His servants, and demonstrates the compassion of the divine law given to humanity through Prophet Muhammad (peace be upon him). God always tells the truth and He says: 'We have sent you as a manifestation of Our grace towards all the worlds.' (21: 107)

It may initially appear that every facility is given to men, but in fact it is given to women at the same time, because sexual pleasure can only be achieved between a man and a woman. This applies even to polygamy. It certainly provides more pleasure to the man who marries more than one wife, but it also gives a chance to a number of women who may have to wait a long time before they have a chance to get married, when marriage is limited to one wife only. There are many religious texts that urge both husband and wife to ensure that the other enjoys sexual pleasure.

The following are texts that encourage a wife to fulfil her husband's right: Abu Hurayrah mentions that God's Messenger (peace be upon him) said: 'If a man calls his wife to bed, but she refuses, the angels will curse her until the morning.' [Related by al-Bukhari and Muslim]

Abu Hurayrah mentions that God's Messenger (peace be upon him) said: 'When a man calls his wife to bed and she refuses, the One in Heaven will be displeased until he is pleased with her.' [Related by Muslim]

Ṭalq ibn ʿAlī narrated that God's Messenger (peace be upon him) said: 'If a man asks his wife to meet his need, she should respond even if she is attending to her baking.' [Related by al-Tirmidhī]

Zayd ibn Arqam said that God's Messenger (peace be upon him) said: 'When a man calls his wife to bed, she should respond even if she is on the back of a camel.' [Related by al-Bazzār]

Other texts encourage a man to fulfil his wife's right. We mentioned these when we discussed shyness and its effect on sexual matters, showing how some female Companions of the Prophet overcame their shyness and spoke about some sexual issues with men who were closely related to their own husbands.

Abu Juhayfah reports: 'The Prophet established the bond of brotherhood between Salman and Abu al-Darda.' Salman visited Abu al-Darda' one day and he found Umm al-Darda' wearing humble clothes. He asked her: "What is wrong?" She said: "Your brother,

Abu al-Darda', does not care for anything in the world." ... Salman said: "Your Lord has a claim against you; your body has a claim against you; and your family has a claim against you. Give everyone their rights." Abu al-Darda' went to see the Prophet and he told him what had happened. The Prophet said: "Salman is right."' [Related by al-Bukhari]

'Abdullāh ibn 'Amr narrated: 'My father married me to a woman of good family. He used to enquire after his daughter-in-law and ask her about her husband. She said: 'He is a fine man who has never been with us in bed and never lifted a cover of ours ever since we have been together.' When this continued for a long time, he mentioned it to the Prophet (peace be upon him). He said: 'Let me meet him.' I later met him, and he asked me: 'How often do you fast?' I said: Every day. He said: 'And how often you recite the Qur'an in full.' I said: Every night... In another version: 'God's Messenger (peace be upon him) said to me: "'Abdullah, I have been informed that you fast every day and offer night worship every night." I said: "This is true, Messenger of God." He said: "Do not do it; but fast on some days and do not fast on others; offer night worship on some nights and do not do so on others. Your body has a claim against you; your eye has a claim against you; your wife has a claim against you...."' [Related by al-Bukhari]

There are several texts that confirm the husband's right and urge the wife to respond quickly. This is due to the fact that by nature, it is the man who seeks and the woman who is sought. He is much more easily excited, and his life activity exposes him to frequent excitement. Hence the Prophet said: 'If any of you sees a woman, let him go to his wife. This will stop what he experiences.' [Related by Muslim] In a different version: 'If any of you admires a woman and finds her appealing, let him go to his wife.' Therefore, the man should make his request gently and the woman should take care of him and respond, even though she may have something else to attend to.

In his voluminous work *Fatḥ al-Bārī*, Imam Ibn Ḥajar says in his commentary on the hadith that says: 'If a man calls his wife to bed...': 'This hadith confirms that man's urge for sexual intercourse is stronger than the woman's, and that it is what distracts his attention most. Therefore, Islam urges women to help men in this regard.' However, in all situations, the main rule in this matter and everything else is the one stated in the Qur'an: 'Women shall, in all fairness, enjoy rights similar to those exercised against them.' (2: 228)

Aspects of facilitating sexual enjoyment

1. Enjoying sex and avoiding pregnancy

Jābir mentions that a man came to see the Prophet (peace be upon him) and said: 'I have a slave woman who serves us and brings our water. I sleep with her, but I do not like her to get pregnant.' The Prophet said: "You may resort to coitus interruptus, if you wish; but whatever is predetermined for her shall happen."' [Related by Muslim]

Jābir narrated: 'We used to resort to coitus interruptus during God's Messenger's lifetime, when the Qur'an was being revealed.' (In Muslim's version: The Prophet was informed but he did not prohibit it.) [Related by al-Bukhari and Muslim]

Al-Bukhari enters this hadith under the chapter heading: coitus interruptus. Imam Ibn Ḥajar said: this means withdrawal, so as to ejaculate without. Abu 'Īsā al-Tirmidhī said: 'A number of scholars among the Prophet's Companions and others said that it is permissible.' Ibn Taymiyyah said: 'As for coitus interruptus, a number of scholars consider it forbidden, but the founders of all four schools of Fiqh said that it is permissible, if the woman agrees.'

2. Permissibility of intercourse during *istiḥāḍah*

'Ikrimah narrated: 'Umm Ḥabībah used to experience prolonged bleeding, i.e. *istiḥāḍah*, and her husband would sleep with her.' [Related by Abu Dāwūd]

Ḥamnah bint Jaḥsh narrated that 'she was in continuous blood discharge, i.e. *istiḥāḍah*, and her husband used to have intercourse with her.' [Related by Abu Dāwūd]

3. Permissibility of enjoying sex, without intercourse, during a woman's period:

Anas narrated: 'When one of their women was menstruating, the Jews would not sit to eat with her and they would not mix with their [menstruating] women in their homes. The Prophet's Companions asked him about this, and God revealed the verse that says: "They ask you about menstruation. Say: 'It is an unclean condition; so keep aloof from women during menstruation, and do not draw near to them until they are cleansed. When they have cleansed themselves, you may go in unto them in the proper way, as God has bidden you. God loves those who turn to Him in repentance, and He loves those who keep themselves pure.'" (2: 222) God's Messenger said [to his Companions]: "You may do everything apart from sexual intercourse." The Jews came to know of this and they said: "This man would not stop until he has differed with every practice we do." Usayd ibn Ḥuḍayr and 'Abbād ibn Bishr came over and said: "Messenger of God, the Jews have said so-and-so. May we have intercourse with them?" The Prophet's face changed colour to the extent that they felt that he was angry with them. They left, and they saw a gift of milk coming to the Prophet. He sent [someone] to call them back, and he gave them a drink. They realized that he was not angry with them.' [Related by Muslim]

Zayd ibn Aslam narrated that a man asked God's Messenger (peace be upon him): 'What is permissible for me when my wife is in menstruation?' The Prophet said: 'Let her tie her lower garment, and you may do what you like with her upper body.' [Related by Mālik]

'Ā'ishah narrated: 'When any of us [the Prophet's wives] was menstruating, God's Messenger (peace be upon him) would tell us to cover our lower part even if we were at the height of our period, then he would have foreplay with us.' She added: 'Who of you can control his desire as God's Messenger (peace be upon him) controlled his desire?' [Related by al-Bukhari and Muslim]

Umm Salamah said: 'I was with the Prophet under a velvet cover when I started my period. I dropped off quietly, picked up my menstruation gear and put it on. God's Messenger (peace be upon him) said to me: "Are you having your period?" I said that I was. He told me to come in and we lay together under the cover.' [Related by al-Bukhari and Muslim]

'Ā'ishah narrated: 'I might drink when I was menstruating, and then hand [the cup over] to the Prophet. He would put his mouth where I placed my mouth, and would drink. I might eat meat off a bone when I was menstruating and then hand it over to the Prophet. He would put his mouth where I placed my mouth.' [Related by Muslim]

Abu Hurayrah said: 'God's Messenger (peace be upon him) was in the mosque when he said: "'Ā'ishah, hand me the garment." She said: "I am menstruating." He said: "Your period is not in your hand." She handed it to him.' [Related by Muslim]

'Ā'ishah said: 'I used to comb God's Messenger's hair when I was menstruating.' [Related by al-Bukhari and Muslim]

4. Permissibility of some enjoyment while doing an act of worship:

While reciting the Qur'an: 'Ā'ishah said: 'God's Messenger (peace be upon him) would recline on my lap when I had my period and he would recite the Qur'an.' [Related by al-Bukhari and Muslim]

When receiving revelations: 'Ā'ishah mentioned that God's Messenger (peace be upon him) said to Umm Salamah: 'Revelations never came to me when I was wearing a woman's garment (in another version: under a woman's cover), except 'Ā'ishah.' [Related by al-Bukhari]

Ablution is not invalidated by a kiss: 'Ā'ishah narrated that 'the Prophet used to kiss his wives, then offer prayers without performing a fresh ablution first.' [Related by al-Nasā'ī]

A kiss or a touch does not spoil fasting: 'Umar ibn al-Khaṭṭāb narrated: 'Feeling joyous, I kissed [my wife] when I was fasting. I said: "Messenger of God, I did today something very serious. I kissed when fasting." He said: "What do you say about rinsing your mouth with water when you are fasting?" I said: It is acceptable. He said: "Then, what?"' [Related by Abu Dāwūd]

Full enjoyment is permissible during the night in Ramadan: God says: 'It is lawful for you to be intimate with your wives during the night preceding the fast. They are as a garment for you, as you are for them.' (2: 187)

During *i'tikāf*, i.e. a long stay in the mosque: 'Alī ibn al-Ḥusayn narrated: 'The Prophet was in the mosque (observing his *i'tikāf*) and his wives were with him, then they left. He said to Ṣafiyyah bint Ḥuyay: "Wait a little so that I come with you." Her home was in Usāmah's house. The Prophet left with her. Two men from the Anṣār met him and looked at the Prophet and went on. The Prophet said to them: 'Come over. This is Ṣafiyyah bint Ḥuyay.' They said: 'Messenger of God! All glory be to Him.' The Prophet said to them: 'Satan could be as close to a man as the blood in his veins. I feared that he might whisper something to you.'" [Related by al-Bukhari]

Washing her husband's head while he is in *i'tikāf*: 'Ā'ishah said: 'God's Messenger would put inside his head to me from the mosque when he was in *ī'tikāf* and I would wash it when I was menstruating.' In a different version, 'Ā'ishah said: 'God's Messenger used to put his head inside for me when I was in my home, and I would comb his hair when I had my period.' [Related by al-Bukhari and Muslim]

During the hajj: Neither a kiss nor a touch invalidates the hajj: In *Bidāyat al-Mujtahid*, Ibn Rushd said: 'The third thing to abandon is sexual intercourse with one's wife. Muslims are unanimous that sexual intercourse is forbidden for a pilgrim from the moment he enters into a state of consecration, i.e. *iḥrām*. This is based on the Qur'anic statement: "While on pilgrimage, a person abstains from lewdness, all wicked conduct and wrangling." (2: 197) The consensus view of scholars is that contact between the two genitals invalidates the hajj.'

In *al-Muḥallā*, Ibn Ḥazm says: 'It is permissible for a person who is in a state of consecration to kiss his wife and enjoy himself with her, provided that he remains short of sexual intercourse. God has only prohibited lewdness, which refers to penetrative intercourse only.'

Preference of performing the hajj in the *tamattu'* method, which allows intimacy with one's wife during the period between finishing the 'umrah and starting the hajj. 'Imrān ibn Ḥuṣayn narrated: 'The verse referring to the *tamattu'* was revealed in God's Book. [This is a reference to the verse that says: "he who takes advantage of performing the 'umrah before the pilgrimage shall make whatever offering he can easily afford." (2: 196)]. We did it when we were with God's Messenger (peace be upon him). No subsequent revelation prohibited it, and the Prophet did not stop it until he passed away.' [Related by al-Bukhari and Muslim]

Jābir mentions: 'We, the Prophet's Companions, started with the declared intention of performing the hajj only, without the ʿumrah... The Prophet (peace be upon him) arrived [in Makkah] on the morning of the fourth of Dhul-Ḥijjah. When we arrived he ordered us to release ourselves from consecration... He was informed that we said: "Now that there are only five days before the Day of Arafat, he is telling us we may consort with our wives. Thus we will go to Arafat with our genitals dripping with semen!'... The Prophet addressed us and said: "You know that I am the most God-fearing among you and the most truthful, seeking what is good for you. Had it not been for that I brought my sacrifice with me, I would have released myself from consecration, as you do. Do it now. Were I to start afresh, I would not bring my sacrifice with me."' We, therefore, released ourselves from consecration in full obedience.' [Related by al-Bukhari and Muslim]

Jābir described the Prophet's pilgrimage in full. He said that after finishing the ʿumrah, the Prophet said: 'Were I to start again, I would not bring my sacrifice with me, and I would have made it an ʿumrah. Those of you who have not brought their sacrifice with them should release themselves from consecration and make this an ʿumrah.' Surāqah ibn Mālik ibn Juʿshum stood up and said: 'Messenger of God, is this for this year of ours or forever?' The Prophet crossed his fingers, putting one next to the other, and said: 'The ʿumrah is incorporated with the hajj, (twice). No, it is forever and ever.'

ʿAlī came from Yemen with the Prophet's camels, and he found that Fāṭimah had released herself from consecration. She wore a coloured dress and applied kohl. He censured her for that. She said: My father ordered me to do it. ʿAlī used to say later in Iraq: I went to God's Messenger (peace be upon him) complaining about Fāṭimah and what she did, seeking his ruling on what she did. I told him that I censured her. He said: 'She told the truth. She told the truth.' [Related by Muslim]

Asmā' bint Abu Bakr narrated: 'We set out in *iḥrām*. God's Messenger (peace be upon him) said: "Whoever has brought his sacrifice stays in *iḥrām*, and those who have not brought a sacrifice release themselves from *iḥrām*." I did not have a sacrifice and therefore I released myself, but al-Zubayr[14] brought his sacrifice with him and he did not release himself.' She said: 'I put on my clothes and came out and sat with al-Zubayr. He said: "Leave me alone." I said: Do you fear that I will jump on you?' [Related by Muslim]

When a pilgrim has performed the *ṭawāf* of *ifāḍah*, the restriction on sexual intercourse is lifted. Scholars are unanimous on this point. They are also in agreement that a pilgrim who has intercourse with his wife before attending at Arafat spoils his hajj. However, they differ on whether the hajj is rendered invalid if one has intercourse after attending at Arafat but before performing the duty of stoning at the 'Aqabah Jamrah, and also on the case of one who does it after stoning at the Jamrah but before performing the *ṭawāf* of *ifāḍah*.

With night worship: It is permissible to have intercourse with one's wife after voluntary night worship. Al-Aswad narrated: 'I asked 'Ā'ishah how did the Prophet offer voluntary prayers during the night. She said: "He used to sleep early at night, then he would wake up late and pray. He then returned to bed. (In Muslim's version, she adds: then if he had need for his wife, he would have it before going to sleep.) When the [Fajr] *adhān* was called, he would rise. He would take a bath if he needed to, or else, he would perform the ablution and go out [to the mosque].' [Related by al-Bukhari and Muslim]

5. Lighter purification after sex

When a person is in a state of ceremonial impurity and wants to go to sleep, he may choose either to take a bath, perform the ablution,

14. Al-Zubayr was her husband.

or resort only to dry ablution. ʿAbdullāh ibn Abi Qays said: 'I asked ʿĀ'ishah: what did the Prophet do concerning purification when he was in the state of ceremonial impurity? Did he take a bath before going to bed, or take a bath when he woke up? She said: 'He did all that. He might take a bath then go to sleep, and he might only perform the ablution and go to sleep.' I said: 'All praise be to God for making things easy for us.' [Related by Muslim]

ʿĀ'ishah narrated: 'When the Prophet wanted to go to bed and he was in a state of ceremonial impurity, he would wash his genitals and perform the ablution as he would perform it for prayer.' [Related by al-Bukhari and Muslim]

Ibn ʿUmar narrated that ʿUmar said: 'Messenger of God, may a person go to sleep when he is in a state of ceremonial impurity?' The Prophet said: 'Yes, if he performs the ablution.' (In another version, he said: Perform the ablution after washing your genitals, then go to bed.) [Related by al-Bukhari and Muslim]

A different version related by Ibn Khuzaymah and Ibn Ḥibbān states: 'Yes, he performs the ablution, if he wishes.'

ʿĀ'ishah said: 'When God's Messenger (peace be upon him) was in a state of ceremonial impurity and he wished to go to sleep, he would perform the ablution, or dry ablution, i.e. *tayammum*.' [Related by al-Bayhaqī]

ʿĀ'ishah narrated: 'God's Messenger (peace be upon him) used to sleep when he was in a state of ceremonial impurity, without touching water.' [Related by al-Tirmidhī]

Dry ablution when water is unavailable

When we look through the texts of the Qur'an and the Sunnah we realize how Islam makes things easy for us when water is unavailable.

A person who has no access to water is not required to abstain from sex with his wife until water is available. He is permitted to resort to dry ablution, i.e. *tayammum*, even if water remains unavailable for some time. God says: 'If you are ill, or travelling, or if one of you has come from the toilet, or if you have cohabited with your wife and can find no water, then have recourse to pure dust, passing therewith lightly over your faces and your hands. God is indeed most lenient, much-forgiving.' (4: 43)

Abu Dharr narrated: 'I did not feel well in Madinah. God's Messenger ordered that I be given a few camels and some sheep. He told me to drink of their milk... I used to be away from water, and my wife was with me. Sometimes, I would be in a state of ceremonial impurity, and I would pray without purifying myself. I went to God's Messenger (peace be upon him), reaching him at midday when he was with a group of his Companions, sitting in the shade of the mosque. He said: 'Abu Dharr?' I said: 'Yes. I am ruined, Messenger of God.' He said: 'What has caused your ruin?' I said: 'I would be away from water, and my wife was with me. I may be in a state of ceremonial impurity and I would pray without purifying myself.' The Prophet (peace be upon him) ordered that some water be brought for me. A black maid brought it, and it was shaking in her hand, in a large jug which was not full. I took cover behind my camel and performed the grand ablution, i.e. *ghusl*, then returned. God's Messenger (peace be upon him) said to me: 'Abu Dharr, pure dust gives adequate purification, even if you remain ten years without water. When water is available to you, wash yourself with it.' [Related by Abu Dāwūd]

When only ablution is needed

Al-Miqdād ibn al-Aswad said: 'I asked God's Messenger (peace be upon him) about a man who approaches his wife and discharges *madhī*. What is he required to do? He said: "If any of you experiences this, let him wash his genital organ with water and perform the ablution, i.e. *wudu*, as he does for prayer."' [Related by Mālik]

Water economy

Anas said: 'God's Messenger (peace be upon him) performed the *ghusl* with one *ṣāʿ* of water or up to five *mudds*, and he performed the ablution with one *mudd*. [A *mudd* is the fill of an average man's two cupped hands. A *ṣāʿ* is equal to four *mudds*. Thus the Prophet performed the *ghusl*, or grand ablution washing all his body with a small amount of water, equal only to four or five *mudds]*

'Ā'ishah narrated: 'When the Prophet (peace be upon him) washed himself to purify himself from ceremonial impurity, he would ask for a large water container and he would take water with his hand, starting washing the right side of his head then the left side.' [Related by al-Bukhari and Muslim]

Abu Salamah narrated: 'I visited 'Ā'ishah together with her brother. Her brother asked her about the Prophet's *ghusl*. She asked for a jug of water containing about one *ṣāʿ*, and performed the *ghusl*, pouring water on her head. There was a screen between her and us.' [Related by al-Bukhari]

Women do not undo their hair

'Ubaydillāh ibn 'Umayr reports: "'Ā'ishah was informed that 'Abdullāh ibn 'Amr used to tell women to undo their hair when they wanted to take a bath to remove ceremonial impurity. She commented: 'I wonder at what this man says, telling women to undo their hair. Why does he not tell them to shave their heads as well? I used to take a bath with the Prophet, using water from the same container, and I would use no more than three handfuls with which I washed my head.'" [Related by Muslim]

Cleaning clothes from semen and menses

'Alqamah and al-Aswad narrated that a man stayed at 'Ā'ishah's place. In the morning, he washed his robe. 'Ā'ishah told him: 'It would have been enough for you to wash the spot if you could see where the semen dropped. If you could not see it, you sprinkle the area with water. I used to rub it off God's Messenger's garment [when it was dry].' [Related by Abu Dāwūd]

'Ā'ishah narrated: 'God's Messenger and I would sleep wearing one garment only, when I would have my period. If a drop [of menses] fell on his garment, he would wash the spot only, without exceeding it.' [Related by Abu Dāwūd]

6. Worship is valid despite some traces of sexual activity

Prayer is valid when one is wearing the same garment used during sexual intercourse. Sulaymān ibn Yasār said: 'I asked 'Ā'ishah about semen falling on one's clothes.' She said: 'I used to wash it off the Prophet's robe and he would go out to prayer, with the effect of the washing clearly apparent as wet spots.' [Related by al-Bukhari and Muslim]

Mu'āwiyah ibn Abi Sufyān narrated that he asked his sister, Umm Ḥabībah, the Prophet's wife: 'Did God's Messenger pray wearing the same garment he was wearing when he had intercourse with her?' She said: 'Yes, he did if he saw nothing on it.' [Related by Abu Dāwūd]

Fasting remains valid if a person starts the day of fasting in a state of ceremonial impurity. Abu Bakr ibn 'Abd al-Raḥmān ibn al-Ḥārith ibn Hishām reported that his father, 'Abd al-Raḥmān, told Marwān that 'Ā'ishah and Umm Salamah informed him that 'God's Messenger (peace be upon him) might be in a state of ceremonial impurity, as a result of being with his wife, then he would take a bath and continue the day fasting.' [Related by al-Bukhari and Muslim]

7. Shortening the period of mourning for all other than one's husband

Umm ʿAṭiyyah narrated: 'We were ordered not to be in mourning for any deceased person for more than three days, except for one's husband: four months and ten days.' [Related by al-Bukhari and Muslim]

That the period of mourning is made so short asserts a husband's right to require his wife to adorn herself and that both enjoy their intimacy together.

8. Shortening the stay away from home

Mālik ibn al-Ḥuwayrith narrated: 'We came to the Prophet, a group of young men of roughly the same age, and stayed with him twenty days and nights. God's Messenger was compassionate and kind. When he felt that we missed our people, he asked us about the families we had left behind and we told him. He said: "Go back to your people and stay with them, teach them and instruct them" – and he mentioned things that I remember or do not remember – "Pray as you have seen me pray. When prayer is due, let one of you say the call to prayer [i.e. the *adhan*], and let your eldest lead the prayer."' [Related by al-Bukhari and Muslim]

9. Marriage termination by husband or wife

God says in the Qur'an: 'Divorce may be [revoked] twice, whereupon a woman may either be retained in fairness or released with kindness. It is unlawful for you to take back from women anything of what you have given them [as dowry], unless they both [husband and wife] fear that they may not be able to keep within the bounds set by God. If you have cause to fear that they would not be able to keep within the bounds set by God, it shall be no offence for either of them if she gives up whatever she may in order to free herself. These are the bounds set by God.' (2: 229)

Ibn ʿAbbās reports: "Thābit ibn Qays ibn Shammās's wife came to the Prophet and said: 'Messenger of God, I do not take anything against Thābit either in his faith or manners, but I fear to be ungrateful.' The Prophet said: 'Are you prepared to give him back his garden?'[15] She said: 'Yes.' She returned the garden to him, and the Prophet ordered Thābit to part with her." [Related by al-Bukhari]

Both ways of terminating a marriage, i.e. divorce and *khul*ʿ which is the termination at the wife's request, open the way for a new marriage, which provides for lawful sexual enjoyment. The desire to terminate the marriage suggests, in most cases, that repeated disagreement between husband and wife deprives them of the intimacy that gives them sexual pleasure.

10. A new marriage for divorcees

Once a divorced woman has finished her waiting period, she is free to enter a new marriage with a different husband. In the case of divorce, the waiting period is short, lasting only for three menstruation periods if the woman is not pregnant, but if she is pregnant, her waiting period ends when she gives birth. God says: 'Divorced women shall wait, by themselves, for three monthly courses.' (2: 228) He also says: 'As for those who are with child, their waiting term shall end when they deliver their burden.' (65: 4)

Fāṭimah bint Qays, one of the early migrants, said that her husband, Abu ʿAmr ibn Ḥafṣ, gave her a final divorce [i.e. a third-time divorce]. She said: 'When I finished my waiting period I told the Prophet that Muʿāwiyah ibn Abi Sufyān and Abu Jahm proposed to marry me.'

15. The woman was appealing to the Prophet to have her marriage terminated. The Prophet's question was to find out whether she was prepared to refund him the dowry he had given her, which in their case was a garden. When she said she was, the Prophet ordered the termination of their marriage.

(In another version: ʿAbd al-Raḥmān ibn ʿAwf and other companions of the Prophet proposed to me). [Related by Muslim]

Fāṭimah bint Qays said that her husband, Abu ʿAmr ibn Ḥafṣ, gave her a final divorce [i.e. a third-time divorce]... She mentioned this to the Prophet, and he said to her: '... When you finish your waiting period, let me know.' When I finished, the Prophet said to me: 'Marry Usāmah ibn Zayd... I married him and God has honoured me by [marrying] him and I was happy with him.' [Related by Muslim]

11. Remarriage of widows

When a woman becomes a widow, she must observe a short waiting period, lasting only four months and ten days if the woman is not pregnant, but if she is pregnant, her waiting period ends when she gives birth. God says: 'Those of you who die leaving wives behind, their wives shall wait, by themselves, for four months and ten days. When they have reached the end of their waiting-term, you shall incur no sin in whatever they may do with themselves in a lawful manner. God is aware of all that you do.' (2: 234)

Subayʿah bint al-Ḥārith, a companion of the Prophet, reports that she was married to Saʿd ibn Khawlah, a companion of the Prophet who took part in the Battle of Badr, but he died during the Prophet's pilgrimage, when she was pregnant. Only a short while after that she gave birth to her child. When she regained her strength, she started to wear make-up expecting a proposal... I went to God's Messenger (peace be upon him) and I asked him. He told me that I have finished my waiting period when I gave birth and he left it up to me to get married if I wished.' (A different version of the hadith mentions that she sought his permission, which he gave her. She subsequently re-married.) [Related by al-Bukhari and Muslim]

CHAPTER V

What Must Be Observed in Enjoying Sex

- One: What to observe in lawful sex
- Two: Manners to help in avoiding unlawful sex
- Three: Manners to observe after committing what is forbidden

What Must Be Observed in Enjoying Sex

The lawful way God has permitted for the satisfaction of sexual desire and enjoying it has made things easy for a Muslim. The values and manners that have to be observed in its fulfilment are easy to implement. They provide the perfect legislation, so that the easy way God has laid down for His servants will ensure the fulfilment of its objectives.

One: What to observe in lawful sex

TIMES WHEN INTERCOURSE IS NOT PERMISSIBLE

During fasting. God says: 'It is lawful for you to be intimate with your wives during the night preceding the fast.' (2: 187) The verse implies that sexual intercourse with one's wife is permissible during the night but not during the time when one is fasting.

During *i'tikāf. I'tikāf* refers to the time when people stay day and night in a mosque, spending their time in various aspects of worship.

God's Messenger says: 'Do not lie with your wives when you are in retreat in the mosques. These are the bounds set by God, so do not come near them. Thus God makes clear His revelations to people, that they may remain God-fearing.' (2: 187)

During *iḥrām* or consecration. God says: 'The pilgrimage takes place in the months appointed for it. Whoever undertakes the pilgrimage in those months shall, while on pilgrimage, abstain from lewdness, all wicked conduct and wrangling.' (2: 197)

During menstruation. God says: 'They ask you about menstruation. Say: "It is an unclean condition; so keep aloof from women during menstruation, and do not draw near to them until they are cleansed. When they have cleansed themselves, you may go in unto them in the proper way, as God has bidden you. God loves those who turn to Him in repentance, and He loves those who keep themselves pure."' (2: 222) This prohibition of 'drawing near' to one's wife during her period refers only to full sexual intercourse. Foreplay and enjoying sexual intimacy that stop short of intercourse are perfectly lawful, as we mentioned earlier, providing the evidence supporting this.

FORBIDDEN PRACTICES:

Anal sex is strictly forbidden, even with one's wife. 'Umar ibn al-Khaṭṭāb said that God's Messenger (peace be upon him) said: 'Steer away from the anus and intercourse during menstruation.' [Related by al-Tirmidhī] Abu Hurayrah said that God's Messenger (peace be upon him) said: 'Cursed is the one who resorts to penetrative sex with his wife in her back.' [Related by Abu Dāwūd] Khuzaymah ibn Thābit said that God's Messenger (peace be upon him) said: 'God does not disapprove of stating the truth, repeating it three times. Do not go into your wives through the anus.' [Related by Ibn Mājah] Sa'īd ibn Yasār said that he said to Ibn 'Umar: 'We buy slave women and we give it sour to them.' He said: 'What does 'giving it sour' mean?' He said: 'Anal sex.' Ibn 'Umar said: 'How disgusting! Does any Muslim do that?' [Related by al-Nasā'ī]

Private marital matters must remain secret. Abu Sa'īd al-Khudrī narrated that God's Messenger (peace be upon him) said: 'One of the worst people in God's sight on the Day of Judgement is a man who is intimate with his wife and she is intimate with him, then he publicizes her secret.' [Related by Muslim]

Asmā' bint Yazīd narrated that she was attending God's Messenger (peace be upon him) with men and women sitting around. He said: 'Perhaps a man may speak about what he does with his wife. And perhaps a woman may tell what she does with her husband.' The people remained silent. I said: 'Yes, indeed, Messenger of God. The women do that, and the men do it, too.' He said: 'Do not do it. It is like a male devil meeting a female devil along a street and copulating with her while people are looking on.' [Related by Ahmad]

Protecting one's honour

Jābir ibn 'Atīq reported that the Prophet (peace be upon him) used to say: 'Some jealousy is loved by God and some He hates. The one which God loves is that confined to real suspicion, while God dislikes jealousy when there is no reason for suspicion.' [Related by Abu Dāwūd]

Proper and sound jealousy imparts strength and courage in defending one's honour, should any attempt of assault occur. As God loves this type of jealousy demonstrated by a Muslim, He honours such a person by giving him the reward of a martyr, should he be killed defending his honour. Sa'īd ibn Zayd narrated that God's Messenger said: 'Whoever is killed defending his property is a martyr; and whoever is killed defending his family is a martyr; and whoever is killed defending his faith is a martyr; and whoever is killed defending his life is a martyr.' [Related by al-Nasā'ī]

Ibn 'Umar said that God's Messenger (peace be upon him) said: 'God shall not look upon three types of people: the one who is undutiful to his parents; the woman who is too masculine in behaviour; and a shameless cuckold.'

Two: Manners to help in avoiding unlawful sex

No description of a woman's beauty. 'Abdullāh ibn Mas'ūd narrated that the Prophet (peace be upon him) said: 'Let not a woman expose another woman, describing her to her own husband as if he is seeing her.' [Related by al-Bukhari]

Covering the *'awrah*: The *'awrah* refers to the area of one's body which is not permissible to expose before other people, except between husband and wife. God says: 'But Satan whispered to them both [i.e. Adam and Eve], so that he might show them their nakedness, of which they had previously been unaware.' (7: 20) 'They both ate of its fruit; and thereupon their shameful parts became visible to them, and they began to cover themselves with pieced-together leaves from the Garden.' (20: 121) 'Children of Adam, We have sent down to you clothing to cover your nakedness, and garments pleasing to the eye.' (7: 26)

God also outlines the following manners to observe in the upbringing of young children: 'Believers! Let those whom you rightfully possess, and those of you who have not yet attained to puberty, ask leave of you at three times of the day: before the prayer of daybreak, and whenever you lay aside your garments in the middle of the day, and after the prayer of nightfall. These are three occasions on which you may happen to be undressed. Beyond these occasions, neither you nor they will incur any sin if they move freely about you, attending to one another. Thus God makes clear to you His revelations. God is all-knowing, wise. Yet when your children attain to puberty, let them ask leave of you, as do those senior to them [in age]. Thus does God make revelations clear to you. God is all-knowing, wise.' (24: 58-59)

Jābir ibn ʿAbdullāh reported that at the time when the Quraysh rebuilt the Kaʿbah, which was about five years before the beginning of Islam and Muhammad became God's Prophet and Messenger, he helped in its rebuilding. He carried the stones of the Kaʿbah which needed to be put back in place. He was wearing his lower garment and carrying the stones on his shoulder. ʿAbbās, his uncle, said to him: 'Nephew, you may as well undo your lower garment and put it on your shoulder to protect it from the stones.' [The Arabs did not wear any underwear at the time] He undid his lower garment and placed it on his shoulder, but he immediately fell unconscious. [Jābir] said: He was never seen naked after that day.' [Related by al-Bukhari and Muslim. This is Muslim's version]

Al-Miswar ibn Makhramah reported: 'I came forward carrying a heavy stone.[16] I was wearing a light lower garment, and it became loose. I could not lay the stone down until I reached the place to put it. God's Messenger (peace be upon him) said to me: "Go back and pick up your garment. None of you may walk naked."' [Related by Muslim]

Abu Saʿīd al-Khudrī narrated that God's Messenger (peace be upon him) said: 'No man may look at another man's *ʿawrah*, nor a woman may look at another woman's *ʿawrah*. No man's body may touch another man's body under the same cover, nor a woman may touch another woman's body under the same cover.' [Related by Muslim]

Staring at a person from the other sex must be avoided. God says: 'Tell believing men to lower their gaze and to be mindful of their chastity. This is most conducive to their purity. God is certainly aware of all that they do. And tell believing women to lower their gaze and to be mindful of their chastity.' (24: 30-31)

16. This incident took place at the time of digging the moat at the entrance to Madinah, to defend it against the forthcoming attack by the Confederate forces.

Needless to say, if staring at a person from the other sex is required to avoid because staring may arouse desire, it behoves us more that men avoid shaking hands with women. Naturally, a touch is a stronger cause of exciting desire than mere looking. Therefore, we should avoid shaking hands with a person from the opposite sex in practically all situations.

Another situation to avoid is mixed play and entertainment. In stressing the need to be serious in mixed society, God says to women: 'Speak in an appropriate manner.' (33: 32). However, seriousness does not contradict a friendly and easy talk. An example is given in the hadith narrated by Abu Mūsā which includes: 'Asmā' bint 'Umays visited Ḥafṣah, the Prophet's wife. Asmā' was one of those Companions of the Prophet who had migrated to Abyssinia in the early years of Islam. 'Umar, [Ḥafṣah's father] entered while Asmā' was still with Ḥafṣah. When he saw her guest he asked Ḥafṣah who was her visitor. She said, 'Asmā' bint 'Umays.' 'Umar said: 'Is she the Abyssinian? Is she the seafarer?' Asmā' confirmed this. 'Umar said to her: 'We were ahead of you in migrating with the Prophet, and thus we have a better claim to him than you.''' [Related by al-Bukhari]

Crowding in mixed places, whether in the street or in social gatherings, must be avoided. Umm Salamah, the Prophet's wife, reports: "When God's Messenger finished his prayers with *salam*, the women would leave straightaway, but he stayed a little while longer before he moved." (Related by al-Bukhari) Ibn Shihāb, an early scholar of high standing, comments: "I think that he stayed on to allow women to leave before those men who also wished to leave early caught up with them." [Related by al-Bukhari]

This is confirmed by the hadith in which the Prophet suggested to his Companions that they should leave a particular door of the mosque to be used only by women. It is further confirmed by the report that the Prophet once left the mosque and noticed that men and women mixed in the street. The Prophet said to the women: 'Stay to one side. It is not up to you to be in the middle of the road. Keep to the sides.' Likewise, mixed crowding should be avoided in places of public meeting. This is achieved by allocating an area in the meeting place for women only, or by taking some other measure to separate men from women.

Private meetings between one man and one woman are not permissible. Ibn 'Abbās narrated that the Prophet said: 'Let no man be alone with one woman unless she is accompanied by a *maḥram*, [i.e a relative who is not permissible for her to marry].' [Related by al-Bukhari]. Imam ibn Ḥajar said: 'This hadith prohibits the presence of one man and one woman alone in an enclosed place. This is unanimously agreed upon, but scholars differ about whether someone else may replace the *maḥram* in such a meeting, such as reliable women. The correct view is that this is permissible.'

Excluded from prohibited private mixed meetings are:

- A necessary private meeting in a public place when other people are present.
- A private meeting between one woman and two or three men, when necessary.
- A meeting of one man with several women.

Imam al-Nawawī said: 'If a man leads the prayer of a congregation of only women who are unrelated to him, in a private place, the majority of scholars say that it is permissible. The evidence is the hadith which says: "As from today, let not a man enter the home of a woman whose husband is absent, unless accompanied by one or two men."' [Related by Muslim] Moreover, it is unlikely that a man can flirt with one woman in the presence of several women.

Women must not try to excite men's desire in any way, including wearing revealing clothes, stepping out with a tempting gait or speaking too softly. God says: 'Do not display your charms as [women] used to display them in the old days of pagan ignorance.' (33: 33) 'Tell believing women... not to display their charms except what may ordinarily appear thereof... Let them not swing their legs in walking so as to draw attention to their hidden charms.' (24: 31) 'Do not speak too softly, lest any who is sick at heart should be moved with desire.' (33: 32)

Three: Manners to observe after committing what is forbidden

We are required to keep our own offences and those of others secret. 'Abdullāh ibn Mas'ūd narrated: 'A man kissed a woman. He came to the Prophet (peace be upon him) and told him. God revealed the verse that says: "Attend to your prayers at both ends of the day and in the early watches of the night. Surely, good deeds erase evil ones." (11: 114) The man asked: 'Is this [verse] for me, Messenger of God?' The Prophet said: 'For everyone of my community who implements it.' [Related by Muslim]

However, a Muslim must not talk about his offences in front of others. Islam recommends that such matters are kept private. The same applies to anyone who sees another committing a sin. The right behaviour is not to publicize the offence. 'Abdullāh ibn Mas'ūd narrated that a man came to the Prophet and said: 'Messenger of God, I flirted with a woman in the far end of Madinah but did not have intercourse with her. Rule in my case as you please.' 'Umar said to him: 'Had you kept it to yourself, God would have given you His shelter.' The Prophet did not say anything to him. So, the man left, but the Prophet sent someone to call him back, and he recited to him the verse that says: "Attend to your prayers at both ends of the day and in the early watches of the night. Surely, good deeds erase evil ones." (11: 114) The man said: 'Messenger of God, does this apply to me?' He said: 'It applies to all people.' [Related by Muslim]

Abu Hurayrah narrated: 'A man came to God's Messenger (peace be upon him) when he was in the mosque and called out saying: "God's Messenger, I have committed adultery." The Prophet turned away from him, until he repeated this four times.' (In Muslim's version: the Prophet said: 'Go back, pray for God's forgiveness and turn to God in repentance.' The man came back a short while later...) [Related by al-Bukhari and Muslim]

Saʿīd ibn al-Musayyib narrated that a man from the clan of Aslam went to Abu Bakr al-Ṣiddīq and said: 'The other [meaning himself] had committed adultery.' Abu Bakr said to him: 'Did you mention this to anyone other than me?' The man said: 'No.' Abu Bakr said: 'Then turn to God in repentance and let the matter remain under God's cover. God accepts His servants' repentance.' [Related by Mālik]

Saʿīd ibn al-Musayyib said: 'I have been told that God's Messenger (peace be upon him) said to a man from the clan of Aslam called Hazāl: "Had you, Hazāl, covered him with your own robe, it would have been better for you."'[17] [Related by Mālik]

The following case is related in al-Ṭabarī's commentary on the Qur'an that a man came to 'Umar and said: 'I had a daughter who was buried alive in pre-Islamic days, but I managed to rescue her before she died. She embraced Islam, but subsequently committed a grave sin. She took a blade to kill herself. I only reached her after she had cut some vein close to her throat. I treated her until she fully recovered. Then she repented well. Now I am receiving proposals of marriage with her. Should I tell the suitor of her past?' 'Umar said to him: 'Do you want to tell of her past? Do you expose what God has

17. This was when Hazāl mentioned to the Prophet that he saw a man committing sinful fornication. The Prophet wanted him not to report it so that it did not become the subject of idle talk.

kept covered? By God, if you tell any person about her past I shall make of you an example for the people of all regions. Give her in marriage like a chaste Muslim woman.'

One aspect of keeping a close cover over sins, whether committed by oneself or others, is that a man marries a woman after having committed adultery with her. Imam Mālik explains this beautifully, as quoted in *al-Mudawwanah al-Kubrā*:

> I asked: Is it proper for a man who has committed adultery with a woman to marry her? Mālik answered: Yes, he should marry her, but should not do so until he has confirmed that she is not pregnant through the adulterous act... Shu'bah, Ibn 'Abbās's *mawlā*, reported that he heard a man asking Ibn 'Abbās: 'I used to follow a woman and I managed to do with her what God has forbidden me. Later, God guided me to turn to Him in repentance. I wanted to marry her, but people quoted me the verse that says: 'The adulterer couples with no one other than an adulteress or an idolatress.' (24: 3) Ibn 'Abbās said: 'This is not what the verse means. Marry her; if there is any sin involved in such a marriage, I bear it.' Ibn Wahb said: 'A number of scholars told me that Mu'ādh ibn Jabal, Jābir ibn 'Abdullāh, Ibn al-Musayyib, Nāfi', 'Abdullāh ibn Mas'ūd, 'Umar ibn 'Abd al-'Azīz and Ḥasan in Muhammad ibn 'Alī ibn Abi Ṭālib said that it is perfectly permissible for him to marry her.' Ibn 'Abbās said that this is a case where the beginning was sinful and the end lawful. God will accept the repentance of anyone who turns to Him in repentance.' Jābir and Ibn al-Musayyib said: 'They started doing what is forbidden and ended doing what is permissible.' Ibn al-Musayyib also said: 'Such a marriage is acceptable if the two people have repented and set their affairs on the right basis, disliking their earlier behaviour.' Ibn Mas'ūd recited: 'It is He who accepts the repentance of His servants and who pardons

> bad deeds. He knows everything you do.' (42: 25) He also says: 'God will indeed accept the repentance of only those who do evil out of ignorance, and then repent shortly afterwards. It is they to whom God turns in His mercy. God is all-knowing, wise.' (4: 17) Therefore, we see nothing wrong with it.[18]

There should be no boasting. Abu Hurayrah narrated: 'I heard God's Messenger (peace be upon him) say: 'Everyone in my community may hope to be forgiven, except those who boast. One aspect of boasting is that a man may do some sin during the night, and it remains unknown in the morning, but he says [to a friend]: "Hey, I did such-and-such last night." His Lord had sheltered him, but he insists on removing God's cover.' [Related by al-Bukhari and Muslim]

No accusation should be made unless there are four witnesses. God says in the Qur'an: 'As for those who accuse chaste women [of adultery], and cannot produce four witnesses, flog them with eighty stripes; and do not accept their testimony ever after; for they are indeed transgressors.' (24: 4)

There should be no circulation of rumours. God says: 'You took it up with your tongues and uttered with your mouths something of which you have no knowledge, thinking it a light matter whereas in God's sight it is grave indeed. If only when you heard it you said: "It is not right for us to speak of this! All glory belongs to You. This is a monstrous slander."' (24: 15-16)

18. Imam Mālik ibn Anas al-Aṣbaḥī, *al-Mudawwanah al-Kubrā*, as narrated by Suḥnūn, Vol. 2, pp. 249-250.

CHAPTER VI

Islamic Law and Aspects of Sexual Enjoyment

- One: Misconceptions that disapprove of lawful sexual enjoyment
- Two: The various forms of permissible sexual pleasure are rewardable for both man and wife
- Three: Love and sexual enjoyment are mutually complementary
- Different levels of sexual enjoyment

Islamic Law and Aspects of Sexual Enjoyment

One: Misconceptions that disapprove of lawful sexual enjoyment

Misconception 1: Sexual intercourse must be only for the purpose of procreation

The fact that divine messages establish a strong link between sexual enjoyment and marriage which leads to the formation of a family that begets sons and daughters has contributed to the misconception that sexual intercourse is permitted only for the purpose of procreation. Its ultimate aim being the preservation of mankind. God has associated it with pleasure and enjoyment in order to encourage people to fulfil this purpose. People who advance this misconception appear to be oblivious of the fact that in animals, the sexual urge becomes active in the great majority of cases during a particular season. Animal mating has a definite purpose, which is procreation and the preservation of species. Had the same been the case with man, God would have given us the same type of urge as He has given animals.

Some people may say that God has made the human sexual instinct greater as a means of test, so that people will show themselves to abide by God's law or not. This argument might have been acceptable had religious directives encouraged man to remain patient in dealing with such a test and ordered abstention from intercourse once pregnancy has been confirmed, until childbirth has occurred and the woman is ready to go through another pregnancy. The fact is that Islam does not give us a single text that refers directly or indirectly to the desirability of such abstention. Instead, the opposite is true: there are numerous texts in the Qur'an and the Sunnah which allow sexual practice for its mere enjoyment, in all situations, including the nights of Ramadan, which is the month of day fasting and night devotion. In the early days of Islam, sexual intercourse was prohibited during the nights of Ramadan, and a number of violations of this prohibition occurred, but then God, in His mercy, permitted it. He says: 'It is lawful for you to be intimate with your wives during the night preceding the fast. They are as a garment for you, as you are for them. God is aware that you have been deceiving yourselves in this respect, and He has turned to you in His mercy and pardoned you. So, you may now lie with them and seek what God has ordained for you.' (2: 187)

Abu Dharr narrated that God's Messenger (peace be upon him) said: '...And [you have] a charity in your intercourse.' People said: 'Messenger of God, would any of us fulfil his desire and still earn a reward for it?' The Prophet said: 'Would he not incur a sin if he does that in an unlawful way?' They said: 'Yes, he does.' The Prophet said: 'Likewise, when he does it in the lawful way, he earns a reward.' [Related by Muslim]

To sum up: Islam confirms that sexual intercourse is always for pleasure, and sometimes for having children. The fact is that God's

Messenger, whose example we are advised to follow and who taught every good thing, continued to have his sexual enjoyment as we shall show in Chapter 7.

Misconception 2: No sex when one's wife is having her period

Muʿādh ibn Jabal mentions: 'I asked God's Messenger (peace be upon him) about what is permissible for a man when his wife is menstruating? He said: "What is above the lower garment, but to refrain from that is better." [Related by Abu Dāwūd] This hadith is markedly lacking in authenticity, and runs contrary to many authentic hadiths which are quoted in Chapter 4 of this volume. We will merely quote one of these hadiths in which the Prophet answers the same question: 'You may do everything except sexual intercourse.'

Misconception 3: One should be shy during sex

To stress this misconception a number of hadiths that are lacking or very poor in authenticity have been circulated, including: Abu Hurayrah narrated from the Prophet: 'When any of you is in intimacy with his wife, he should cover himself. If he does not, the angels will feel shy and leave, while Satan will be present. If the intercourse results in conception, Satan will have a share in that child.' [Related by al-Ṭabarānī] Ibn Masʿūd narrated from the Prophet: 'When any of you is in intimacy with his wife, he should cover himself. They should not be naked like two asses.' [Related by al-Ṭabarānī] 'Ā'ishah narrated: 'I never looked at or saw God's Messenger's genitals.' [Related by Ibn Mājah]

Moreover, a number of false and fabricated hadiths have been circulated, such as: 'Ibn 'Abbās narrated from the Prophet: 'When any of you has sexual intercourse with his wife or his slave woman, let him not look at her genital, because it may cause blindness.' [Related by Ibn 'Adiy] 'Abu Hurayrah narrated from the Prophet: 'When any of you has intercourse, he should not look at the genital area because it may cause blindness. He should not say much, because it may cause dumbness.' [Related by al-Daylamī]

These hadiths that are either lacking in authenticity or are totally fabricated are contrary to many authentic hadiths, of which we will cite only one: Ḥakīm narrated from his father: 'I said: Messenger of God, what may we do and refrain from doing concerning our *'awrah* [i.e. private parts]? He said: "Cover your *'awrah* except with your wife or what your hand possesses."' [Related by Abu Dāwūd]

Ibn Ḥazm said: 'How strange it is that some ignorant people permit copulation but prohibit looking at the genital organ. It is sufficient to quote in this respect what God says in describing the believers: "Who refrain from sex except with those joined to them in marriage, or those whom they rightfully possess – for then, they are free of all blame." Thus, God, Mighty and Exalted, commands refrain except between spouses. He states that there is no blame in that, and this is a general statement that covers looking, touching and penetration.'[19]

Misconception 4: Female circumcision

In order to stress the merit of the alleged virtue of restraint and to limit the chances of enjoying sexual pleasure for both men and women, the notion that girls must be circumcised was widely held in some Muslim countries for many centuries. Thus, it was wrongly thought that female circumcision was an Islamic duty and ignoring it left a stigma on the girl, while doing it was honourable for the girl. All this is an unfounded misconception. The misconception was supported by a widely circulated hadith that is very poor in authenticity: Shaddād ibn Aws said that the Prophet (peace be upon

19. Ibn Ḥazm, *al-Muḥallā*, Vol. 10, p. 33.

him) said: 'Circumcision is a recommended sunnah for males and an act of goodness for females.' [Related by al-Ṭabarānī]

The fact is that female circumcision was a habit in Arabian society in pre-Islamic days. Islam attached to it clear conditions that reduced its effects on both men and women, while maintaining their rights to enjoy sex. Umm 'Aṭiyyah of the Anṣār reported that one of the women in Madinah used to circumcise girls. The Prophet said to her: 'Do not exaggerate, so that it remains more pleasing for the woman and better enjoyed by her husband.' [Related by Abu Dāwūd] Another version related by al-Ṭabarānī mentions that the Prophet said to that woman: 'Take off a little, but do not exaggerate, so that its [effect] is better in appearance and more pleasing to the husband.'

In his priceless work *Fiqh al-Sunnah*, Sayyid Sābiq said: 'The hadiths suggesting female circumcision are all poor in authenticity. None of them is authentic.'[20]

Two: The various forms of permissible sexual pleasure are rewardable for both man and wife

Sexual intercourse between man and wife is not permitted only for procreation and having children. It is permitted, first and last, for healthy pleasure and enjoyment. To seek such enjoyments, without the desire to have children, is perfectly legitimate. Indeed it is a sunnah done by the Prophet (peace be upon him) and should be emulated. Moreover, it is a recommended practice which earns reward for the person who does it, as clearly stated in the hadith mentioned at the beginning of this chapter, in which the Prophet says: '...And [you have] a charity in your intercourse.' Moreover, all levels of

20. Female circumcision is unknown in most Muslim countries. It is confined to some parts of Arabia and a number of countries in central Africa, many of which have a non-Muslim majority.

sexual activity between man and wife are among the pleasures of this present life, as God says: 'Alluring to man is the enjoyment of worldly desires through women and offspring, heaped-up treasures of gold and silver, horses of high mark, cattle and plantations. These are the comforts of this life. With God is the best of all goals.' (3: 14) Perhaps this Qur'anic verse makes sexual enjoyment as the first and most pleasing of all life pleasures. The Prophet himself highlights this: 'Abdullāh ibn 'Amr quotes the Prophet as saying: "The life of this world is but a source of enjoyment, and the best source of enjoyment in this life is a good woman." [Related by Muslim]

Of all pleasures of life, the ones that were dear to God's Messenger (peace be upon him) were women and perfume. Anas quotes God's Messenger as saying: 'What has been made appealing to me in this life of yours are women and perfume. But the dearest thing that gives me satisfaction is prayer.' [Related by al-Nasā'ī]

Thus a Muslim couple are free to partake of all that pleases them of permissible enjoyment, as they may fancy. Moreover, they may peruse such practices in books that deal with this subject in a serious and scientific way. They should be fully aware of the two forbidden practices: anal intercourse at all times and frontal intercourse during the woman's menstruation. Apart from that, there is no problem with trying anything known, or will be known, to human beings, provided that it is not harmful. This is based on the great and fundamental rule of Islamic law: 'Things are initially permissible, except for what the Shariah states to be forbidden.' However, in this context, we should highlight a recommended Islamic practice, i.e. sunnah, which is also essential to proper and healthy human life. We are referring here to moderation. Moderation applies to all permissible things. God says in the Qur'an: 'Children of Adam... Eat and drink but do not be wasteful. Surely, God does not love the wasteful.' (7: 31) Indeed, moderation is required when we attend to our worship. The Prophet (peace be upon him) said to 'Abdullāh ibn

ʿAmr: "ʿAbdullah, I have been informed that you fast every day and offer night worship every night." I said: "This is true, Messenger of God." He said: "Do not do it; but fast on some days and do not fast on others; offer night worship on some nights and do not do so on others."

Three: Love and sexual enjoyment are mutually complementary

Within marriage, love is a component of a complete whole. Let us say that marriage means mutual love, as God says: 'And among His signs is that He creates for you spouses out of your own kind, so that you might incline towards them, and He engenders love and tenderness between you.' (30: 21) Love ensures a faithful relationship based on good and pleasant companionship as well as full life partnership. It is as Imam Ibn al-Qayyim describes: 'Intercourse with your loved wife does not weaken your body, yet it discharges plenty of semen, while intercourse with a woman you dislike saps your strength and discharges little semen.'[21]

Certain practices help to ensure full sexual enjoyment. The first of these is to say a supplication and mention God's name before the couple start. Ibn ʿAbbās reports that the Prophet (peace be upon him) said: 'When a person is about to have intercourse with his wife he should say: "My Lord, keep Satan away from us and keep him away from what You give us." If he does and a child is given them as a result, Satan shall never harm it.' [Related by al-Bukhari and Muslim]

Secondly, both husband and wife should attend to their appearance, putting on something to please the other. This is particularly encouraged for women: ʿAbdullāh ibn Sallām narrated that the

21. Ibn al-Qayyim, *Zād al-Maʿād*, Cairo, 1989, Vol. 3, p. 239.

Prophet said: 'The best of women is one who pleases you when you look at her.' [Related by al-Ṭabarānī]

Abu Juḥayfah narrated from his father: 'The Prophet established a bond of brotherhood between Salmān and Abu al-Dardā.' Once Salmān went to visit Abu al-Dardā' and saw his wife wearing plain clothes. He asked her the reason and she told him: "Your brother, Abu al-Dardā', does not care for anything in this life."' [Related by al-Bukhari]

'Ā'ishah narrated: "Uthmān ibn Maẓ'ūn's wife used to wear henna and perfume, but then abandoned this. She visited me, and I said to her: "What is wrong with you?" She said: "'Uthmān does not care for this life and does not care for women." (A different version related by al-Ṭabarānī mentions that the Prophet met 'Uthmān and said to him: "'Uthmān, are you not required to follow my example?")... "Your family has a claim on you and your body has a claim on you"... She visited them later wearing adornments like a bride. They asked her: "How come?" She said: "We have experienced what other people have experienced."' [Related by Ahmad]

Jābir ibn 'Abdullāh narrated: "Alī came from Yemen with the Prophet's camels, and he found that Fāṭimah had released herself from consecration. She wore a coloured dress and applied kohl. He censured her for that. She said: "My father ordered me to do it."' [Related by Muslim]

Anas ibn Mālik reports that he saw Umm Kulthūm, the Prophet's daughter, wearing a cloak with silk stripes. [Related by al-Bukhari]

Subay'ah, a companion of the Prophet, mentions that when she regained her strength after having given birth, 'she put on makeup, hoping for a marriage proposal.' [Related by al-Bukhari and Muslim] Another version related by Ahmad mentions that 'she applied kohl and henna and attended to her appearance.' If a Companion of the Prophet wears makeup, including kohl and henna, hoping for a new proposal of marriage, we feel that a wife should be more attentive to her appearance and wear better makeup when she is with her husband.

Jābir ibn 'Abdullāh narrated: 'We returned with the Prophet (peace be upon him) after a military expedition... When we were about to enter Madinah, he said: "Stay back so that you go home in the evening, allowing the woman with dishevelled hair to comb her hair, and the one whose husband has been away attend to her toilet.' [Related by al-Bukhari and Muslim]

'Ā'ishah narrated: 'We used to come out with God's Messenger (peace be upon him) to Makkah and we would wrap on our foreheads perfumed bands.' [Related by Abu Dāwūd]

Umaymah bint Ruqayqah narrated that 'the Prophet's wives used to have bands perfumed with *warss* and saffron, tying their hair so that it did not drop on their foreheads.' [Related by al-Ṭabarānī]

'Imrān ibn Ḥuṣayn narrated that the Prophet (peace be upon him) said: 'Women's makeup is a colour without scent.' Sa'īd [one of the narrators of this hadith] said: 'I think that they understood that what the Prophet said about women's makeup applied to the time when she went out. When she is with her husband, she may wear whatever makeup she likes.' [Related by Abu Dāwūd]

Anas ibn Mālik reports about his mother, Umm Sulaym: 'When her husband came in, she gave him a good dinner. Then after the meal, she put on her best appearance, and he made love to her.' [Related by al-Bukhari and Muslim]

Attending to one's appearance equally applies to men. God says: 'Women shall, in all fairness, enjoy rights similar to those exercised against them.' (2: 228) In his commentary on the Qur'an, al-Ṭabarī quotes Ibn ʿAbbās: 'I like to adorn myself for my wife in the same way as I like her to adorn herself for me, because God, the Exalted, said: "Women shall, in all fairness, enjoy rights similar to those exercised against them."' As Ibn ʿAbbās attends to his appearance when he is with his wife in order to implement this Qur'anic statement, we think that he should do it also to implement the Prophet's statement: 'Your family has a claim on you.' The right of the family has several dimensions, including that of attending to appearance. Needless to say, a man may attend to his appearance in a way that befits the most noble of people. The one at the top grade of all mankind is Prophet Muhammad (peace be upon him), and he used to attend to his appearance. Here are some examples:

Al-Barā' ibn ʿĀzib narrated: 'I saw the Prophet (peace be upon him) wearing a red suit which was the best I had ever seen.' [Related by al-Bukhari and Muslim] Anas reports: 'The *ḥibarah*, [which is a Yemeni type of cloak], was the type of garment the Prophet liked best.' [Related by al-Bukhari and Muslim] In *Fatḥ al-Bārī*, Imam Ibn Ḥajar says that the *ḥabarah* is a type of Yemeni cloak made of cotton. Yemeni people considered it their best type of clothing. Al-Qurṭubī said that it was called *ḥibarah*, deriving the name from a root that meant wearing adornments.

ʿĀ'ishah narrated that the Prophet used to start with the right side whenever he could, including combing the hair of his head and beard. In another version she said that she used to comb the Prophet's head. [Related by al-Bukhari and Muslim]

Ibn ʿAbbās narrated that 'the Prophet used to let his hair drop over his forelock, but subsequently he used to part it.' [Related by al-Bukhari and Muslim]

ʿĀ'ishah reported: 'I used to apply perfume to God's Messenger (peace be upon him), using the best I could find.' In another version related by Muslim: 'using perfume that included musk.'

Ibn 'Umar reported that the Prophet used to inhale the vapour of aloe vera and *kāfūr*. [Related by Muslim]

Another practice of attending to appearance is the removal of pubic hair. Abu Hurayrah said: 'I heard the Prophet (peace be upon him) say: "Five things are part of sound human nature: circumcision, shaving pubic hair, trimming one's moustache, clipping one's nails, and plucking armpit hair.' [Related by al-Bukhari]

Jābir ibn 'Abdullāh narrated: 'We returned with the Prophet (peace be upon him) after a military expedition... When we were about to enter Madinah, he said: "Stay back so that you go home in the evening, allowing the woman with dishevelled hair to comb her hair, and the one whose husband has been away attend to her toilet.' [Related by al-Bukhari and Muslim]

A fourth practice is taking care of the sensitive parts of one's body by both husband and wife. As far as the man is concerned, we have just mentioned the hadith in which the Prophet speaks of five things as part of sound human nature. The first of these is 'circumcision.' Male circumcision removes the skin that covers the tip of the man's genital organ. This tip is very sensitive and gives the man greater pleasure on touch.

Female circumcision is the opposite, because it results in less enjoyment. We have stated that the hadith that describes it as a good thing for the woman is not authentic. On the contrary, there are hadiths warning parents who want to have their daughters circumcised that they must not exaggerate that. They should keep it gentle. We have discussed this aspect in greater detail when we discussed the misconceptions about sexual enjoyment.

The last recommended practice applies to a man who wants to have a second intercourse. It is recommended that he takes a shower or performs the ablution before it. Abu Sa'īd al-Khudrī said that God's

Messenger (peace be upon him) said: 'If any of you has had sexual intercourse with his wife and wants a repeat, he should perform the ablution.' (Ibn Khuzaymah adds in another version: It is fresher for a repeat.) [Related by Muslim]

Different levels of sexual enjoyment

We may identify four levels of sexual enjoyment. The first of these is the enjoyment of companionship between man and wife. This may be manifested in different situations, one of these is playing and having fun together. Jābir ibn 'Abdullāh reports: 'God's Messenger asked me: "Jābir, have you got married?" I said: "Yes." He asked: "A virgin or a mature woman?" I said: "She is a mature woman." He said: "Would it not have been better for you to marry a young one: you would play with her and she would play with you; and you have fun together?" I said to him: "'Abdullāh has died leaving behind several daughters, and I did not want to bring them one like them. I thought it better to bring them a mature woman who would take care of them and their upbringing." He said: "May God bless you."' [Related by al-Bukhari and Muslim]

'Ā'ishah reports: 'I went on a journey with the Prophet when I was still young and slim, having put on no extra weight. He said to the people with us: "Go ahead." They went ahead of us. He then said to me: "Let us race." We raced and I won. He did not say anything. Later, when I had put on weight and forgot the incident, I went with him on a journey. He again said to the people with us: "Go ahead," and they went ahead of us. He said to me: "Come, let us race." I said: "How can I race you, Messenger of God, when I am in this condition?" He said: "You can do it." We raced and he won. He smiled and said: "One for one."' [Related by Ahmad]

'Ā'ishah reports: 'God's Messenger (peace be upon him) shielded me with his upper garment when I watched the Abyssinians doing their folklore play in the mosque. I remained so until I had enough. You should give allowances to a young woman who is keen to have fun.' [Related by al-Bukhari and Muslim]

Another situation that testifies to how gentle the Prophet was with his wives is described by 'Ā'ishah who said: 'I might drink when I was menstruating, and then hand [the cup over] to the Prophet. He would put his mouth where I placed my mouth, and would drink. I might eat meat off a bone when I was menstruating and then hand it over to the Prophet. He would put his mouth where I placed my mouth.' [Related by Muslim]

Closer situations are reported by 'Ā'ishah: 'We accompanied God's Messenger (peace be upon him) on some of his travels... Abu Bakr came over to me while God's Messenger had placed his head on my thigh and slept. He said: "You have stopped God's Messenger when the people are near no water spring and they have no water" ... Abu Bakr remonstrated with me, and he poked me on my waist. Nothing stopped me from moving except the fact that God's Messenger's head was on my thigh.' [Related by al-Bukhari and Muslim]

'Ā'ishah said: 'God's Messenger (peace be upon him) would recline on my lap when I had my period and he would recite the Qur'an.' [Related by al-Bukhari and Muslim]

'Ā'ishah reports: 'It was the Day of Eid, and the Africans played with leather shields and spears. Either I asked the Prophet, or he said to me: "Do you like to watch?" I said: "Yes." He put me behind him, with my cheek on his cheek. He said to them: "Carry on, People of Arfidah." When I had had enough, he asked me: "Have you had enough?" I said: "Yes." He then said: "You may go."' [Related by al-Bukhari and Muslim]

'Ā'ishah narrated that she used to comb the Prophet's hair when he was in *i'tikāf* in the mosque. He would put his head through to her as she was in her apartment. [Related by al-Bukhari and Muslim]

The second level is that of light sexual enjoyment, such as a kiss, hug or touch. Umm Salamah narrated that 'the Prophet used to kiss her when he was fasting.' [Related by al-Bukhari]

'Umar ibn al-Khaṭṭāb narrated: 'Feeling joyous, I kissed [my wife] when I was fasting. I said: "Messenger of God, I did today something very serious. I kissed when fasting." He said: "What do you say about rinsing your mouth with water when you are fasting?" I said: It is acceptable. He said: "Then, what?" [Related by Abu Dāwūd]

Abu al-Naḍr mentions that 'Ā'ishah bint Ṭalḥah[22] was with 'Ā'ishah [the Prophet's wife] when her own husband ['Abdullāh] ibn 'Abd al-Raḥmān ibn Abu Bakr. 'Ā'ishah said to him: 'What stops you from coming close to your wife, speaking to her and kissing her?' He said: 'Would I kiss her when I am fasting?' She said: 'Yes.' [Related by Mālik in *al-Muwaṭṭa.*']

The third level is foreplay. One aspect of this is sucking the tongue and lips of one's wife. Jābir ibn 'Abdullāh narrated that he got married. 'God's Messenger (peace be upon him) asked me: "What sort of woman did you marry?" I said: "I married a previously married woman." He said: "You miss out on a virgin and her watering mouth."' [Related by al-Bukhari]

Imam Ibn Ḥajar referred to the last word in the Prophet's statement, translated here as 'her watering mouth.' He said: 'Most scholars read this word as *li'ābihā*, which means "and foreplay." Yet in a different version it is read as *lu'ābihā*,[23] meaning 'her saliva.' This is a reference

---

22. 'Ā'ishah bint Ṭalḥah was 'Ā'ishah's niece. Her mother was Umm Kulthūm bint Abu Bakr. Her father was Ṭalḥah ibn 'Ubaydullāh, one of the earliest Companions of the Prophet.
23. Both versions are written in the same way. The difference is in the diacritics, which are normally not written except where one wants to inform of the right pronunciation.

to sucking one's wife's lips and tongue when kissing her. It is a probable meaning as al-Qurṭubī suggests.'

'Utbah ibn 'Uwaym ibn Sā'idah al-Anṣārī narrated, from his father, from his grandfather, that God's Messenger (peace be upon him) said: 'Choose virgin women. They have sweeter mouths, give you more children and are satisfied with little.' [Related by Ibn Mājah]

Hugging is another aspect of foreplay. Zayd ibn Aslam narrated that a man asked God's Messenger (peace be upon him): 'What is permissible for me when my wife is menstruating?' The Prophet said: 'Let her tie her lower garment, and you may do what you like with her upper body.' [Related by Mālik]

Ḥarām ibn Ḥakīm's uncle asked God's Messenger: 'What is permissible for me when my wife is menstruating?' He said: 'Her body that is above her lower garment.' [Related by Abu Dāwūd]

Foreplay may also include sucking one's wife's breast. Yaḥyā ibn Sa'īd mentions that a man asked Abu Mūsā al-Ash'arī, saying: 'I sucked some milk from my wife's breast and I swallowed it.' Abu Mūsā said: 'I think that she is now forbidden to you.' 'Abdullāh ibn Mas'ūd said to him: 'Think carefully of what ruling you are giving the man?' Abu Mūsā asked him: 'What do you say on this?' 'Abdullāh ibn Mas'ūd said: 'There is no breastfeeding except when the child is in its first two years of age.' Abu Mūsā said: 'Do not ask me about anything as long as this eminent scholar is among you.' [Related by Mālik]

The fourth level of sexual enjoyment is intercourse. Each of the three levels we have mentioned may have its time and separate occasion, but they also may be a prelude to this fourth level of full intercourse. The Prophet teaches us to be gentle and to allow preliminaries to sexual intercourse, to make it an occasion of real enjoyment. Jābir ibn 'Abdullāh reports: 'God's Messenger (peace be upon him) said to me: "Have you got married?" I said: Yes. He said... "When you are with her, be gentle; be gentle."' [Related by al-Bukhari and Muslim] Thus, the Prophet instructs Jābir, a young man, in the early period of his married life, to be gentle with his wife, and to approach her with some fun and play.

As long as intercourse is in the woman's vagina, she may be approached from any direction. Jābir said that the Jews used to say that when a man approaches his wife from the rear, their child will be cross-eyed. God then revealed the verse that says: 'Your wives are your tilth; go, then, to your tilth as you may desire, but first provide something for your souls.' (2: 223) [Related by al-Bukhari and Muslim]

Ibn 'Abbās said: 'Prior to Islam, the Anṣār worshipped idols, while the Jews were a community with divine revelations. The Anṣār used to consider the Jews to be more learned, and they emulated many of their practices. It was the practice of the people of earlier revelations that they approached their wives when they were well covered. The Anṣār followed their suit. The Quraysh people, on the other hand, used to have their wives undressed and to enjoy them from the front, rear and lying on their backs. When the Muhājrīn came to Madinah, one man married an Anṣārī woman. He wanted to do this with her, but she refused. She said: "We are used to being covered when approached. Do that or leave me alone." Their disagreement continued and God's Messenger (peace be upon him) was informed. Then God revealed the verse that says: Your wives are your tilth; go, then, to your tilth as you may desire, but first provide something for your souls.' [Related by Abu Dāwūd]

Umm Salamah reported: 'When the Muhājirīn came to Madinah, they married women from the Anṣār. The Muhājirīn used to approach their wives as they were lying on their tummies, while the Anṣār did not do that. One man from the Muhājirīn wanted to do that with his wife, but she refused until she asked God's Messenger (peace be upon him). She went to him, but she felt too shy to put her question to him. Umm Salamah asked him instead. God then revealed: "Your wives are your tilth; go, then, to your tilth as you may desire, but first provide something for your souls."' [Related by Ahmad]

Ibn 'Abbās narrated that 'Umar came to God's Messenger and said: 'Messenger of God, I am ruined.' The Prophet asked him: 'What has ruined you?' He said: 'I took my mount the other side last night.' The Prophet did not give any answer. Then God's Messenger received this verse as it was revealed to him: Your wives are your tilth; go, then, to your tilth as you may desire, but first provide something for your souls.' [Related by al-Tirmidhī] This means that one may approach his wife from either side, provided that it is a frontal intercourse.

It is also permissible to see one's spouse in the nude. Maymūnah narrated: 'I placed water for the Prophet's bath. He washed his hand twice or three times, then he poured some water on his left hand and washed his genital. (In another version: he washed his genital and any stains). He then rubbed his hand on the floor, then rinsed his mouth, inhaled water, washed his face and arms, then poured water over all his body. He then changed position and washed his feet.' [Related by al-Bukhari and Muslim]

'Ā'ishah narrated: 'When God's Messenger (peace be upon him) wanted to take a bath, he started with his right hand, pouring water on it to wash it. He then poured water on any stains on his right hand and removed them with his left hand. When he did that, he poured water on his head... I used to take a bath with God's Messenger, when we both were in the state of ceremonial impurity, using the water in a single container.' [Related by al-Bukhari and Muslim]

Imam Ibn Ḥajar said that al-Dāwūdī quoted this hadith of 'Ā'ishah and said in relation to her statement, 'I used to take a bath with God's Messenger using the water in a single container.' He considered it evidence that it is permissible for husband and wife to look at each other's *'awrah*. This is confirmed by Ibn Ḥibbān's narration through Sulaymān ibn Mūsā that he was asked about the case of a husband looking at his wife's genitals. He said: 'I asked 'Aṭā' and he told me that he asked 'Ā'ishah. She mentioned this hadith in meaning. It is a clear text that is relevant to the question, but God knows best.'

Ḥakīm narrated from his father: I said: 'Messenger of God, what may we do regarding our *'awrah*, and what we must not do?' He said: 'Keep your *'awrah* covered, except with your wife or what your right hand possesses.' [Related by Abu Dāwūd]

Another aspect is that both husband and wife use the same container when taking a bath. Maymūnah mentioned that she used to take a bath with the Prophet, using the water from the same container. [Related by Muslim]

Umm Salamah narrated: 'I used to take a bath with the Prophet using water from the same container.' Another version related by al-Nasā'ī mentions that Umm Salamah was asked: 'May a woman take a bath with her husband?' She said: 'Yes, if she is well behaved. I used to take a bath with the Prophet using water from the same container.' [Related by al-Bukhari and Muslim]

'Ā'ishah narrated: 'I used to take a bath with God's Messenger, when we both were in the state of ceremonial impurity, using the water in a single container. He would take some and I would say: Leave some for me; leave some for me.' [Related by Muslim]

Thus, a married couple may complete the pleasure of intercourse with enjoying a shared bath. It is a pleasant end for the perfect sexual enjoyment God has given to His servants.

CHAPTER VII

The Prophet's Guidance on Marriage and Enjoyment

- Foreword: Why are we too sensitive about the Prophet's enjoyment of sex?
- Striking a balance between enjoyable marriage and aspiration for the best
- Aspiring to what is best in worship
- Special privileges for Prophets: a continuous and miraculous tradition
- The Prophet's special privileges in marriage and enjoyment
- How the Prophet enjoyed sex

The Prophet's Guidance on Marriage and Enjoyment

Foreword: Why are we too sensitive about the Prophet's enjoyment of sex?

If we betray an attitude of exaggerated sensitivity concerning sexual enjoyment generally, such sensitivity is far greater when this concerns the Prophet (peace be upon him). We all know that the Sunnah covers everything that we learn from the Prophet, in word, deed or approval. This means that what he did to enjoy himself is a part of the Sunnah. The Prophet was keen to teach Muslims everything that was of use to them in their lives. The unbelievers noted this and even spoke about it. Salmān narrated: 'The unbelievers said to us: "Your Prophet teaches you everything, even defecation?" He said to them: "Yes, he taught us not to clean ourselves with our right hands, and not to face the *qiblah* when we go to the toilet. He told us not to use animal drippings or bones to cleanse ourselves. He also said that we should use at least three solid objects[24] when cleansing ourselves.' [Related by Muslim]

A contributing factor to such sensitivity about the Prophet and sexual enjoyment is the attitude of Orientalists in our modern times. They question this at length, and their questioning is based on their Christian concept that suggests that a human being can only rise in spirituality through being contemptuous of worldly desires, particularly that surrounding sexuality. They say: how can a Messenger of God enjoy sex in a greater degree than other ordinary Muslims? This is a reference to the fact that the Prophet was married to nine wives. This criticism by latter day Orientalists is an echo of that raised by the Jews during the Prophet's lifetime.

In his commentary on the Qur'an, al-Ṭabarī quotes Ibn ʿAbbās who says: 'The people of earlier revelations said: Muhammad claimed that he was given his message with no aspiration on his part. Yet he has nine wives, and his only interest is sex. Which king is better placed than him? Refuting what they claimed God revealed in the Qur'an: 'Do they, perchance, envy other people for what God has given them out of His bounty? We have indeed given revelation and wisdom to the House of Abraham, and We did bestow on them a mighty dominion.' (4: 54)

Striking a balance between enjoyable marriage and aspiration for the best

God gave His Messenger a number of special privileges, and one of these was that of marriage, which involves sexual enjoyment. However, God coupled these special privileges with giving him a number of great characteristics that apply only to His messengers

24. The literal translation of the word used in the hadith is 'stone', but what is meant is 'solid object', such as toilet paper. It is preferable to also add washing with water.

endowed with strong will and resolve. All these characteristics tend to motivate a continuous aspiration to what is superior. Before we present some examples of the Prophet's aspiration for the best, whether in choosing his wives or during his life with them, we mention two examples of his directives to his Companions to seek what is best.

The first example is that he urged his Companions to seek what is superior when choosing a wife. Abu Hurayrah narrated that the Prophet (peace be upon him) said: 'A woman is sought in marriage for any of four qualities: her wealth, lineage, beauty and religion. Make sure to choose the one who is religious.' [Related by al-Bukhari and Muslim]

The other example is noted in his prayer to God to bless his Companion when he showed that he preferred the better option. Jābir ibn 'Abdullāh reports: 'God's Messenger asked me: "Jābir, have you got married?" I said: "Yes." He asked: "A virgin or a mature woman?" I said: "She is a mature woman." He said: "Would it not have been better for you to marry a young one: you would play with her and she would play with you; and you have fun together?" I said to him: "'Abdullāh has died leaving behind several daughters, and I did not want to bring them one like them. I thought it better to bring them a mature woman who would take care of them and their upbringing." He said: "May God bless you."' [Related by al-Bukhari and Muslim]

We will look in brief on some of his marriages to show how he looked for the best when choosing every one of his wives. Thus, the aspiration for the best was always coupled with the natural desire to marry and enjoy marital life. 'Ā'ishah was chosen by God to be his wife. Yet what encouraged such a marriage is the fact that she was the daughter of his best friend and Companion, Abu Bakr al-Ṣiddīq. The Prophet said about him: 'Were I to choose a bosom friend, I would have chosen Abu Bakr. Rather, he is my brother and Companion.' The Prophet's marriage with his daughter was a gesture of honour to that Companion. Honouring one's friends is a noble action.

His marriage to Umm Salamah was to console a devout woman who had migrated to Abyssinia, then to Madinah, enduring much hardship. She then observed what Islam requires and did not lament the loss of her husband, much as she loved him. Umm Salamah narrated: 'When my husband, Abu Salamah, died, I thought: "He died a stranger in a foreign land. I will lament his departure in a way that people will continue to speak about for long." I prepared myself for such lamentation and a woman from the upper parts of Madinah came over, wanting to join me in my lamentation. The Prophet met her and said: "Do you want to bring Satan into a home when God has already driven him out?" He said this twice. On hearing this, I refrained from lamentation.' [Related by Muslim]

Umm Salamah was faithful to her first husband's memory. She said: 'I heard God's Messenger (peace be upon him) say: "If a calamity befalls a Muslim and he says what God has ordered him to say: 'We all belong to God and to Him we shall all return. My Lord, reward me for my calamity and grant me what is better than my loss,' God is certain to give him what is better."' Umm Salamah said: 'When Abu Salamah died, I thought: who among the Muslims is better than Abu Salamah? He was the first to migrate with his family in order to be with God's Messenger. Anyway, I said it and God granted me God's Messenger as my husband.' [Related by Muslim]

The Prophet married Ḥafṣah bint 'Umar after she became a widow. This was a gesture of honour to 'Umar who was instrumental in declaring God's Message openly in Makkah, after it had been advanced in secret. His standing with God's Messenger was second only to Abu Bakr.

Umm Ḥabībah was another wife of the Prophet. She was among the first to migrate to Abyssinia with her husband. There her husband converted to Christianity, but she was firm in her faith, continuing with her migration.

His marriage to Ṣafiyyah bint Ḥuyay ibn Akhṭab deserves more reflection. She was pretty and the daughter of the chief of the Jewish tribe of al-Naḍīr. Her husband was killed in the Battle of Khaybar. As captive, she was assigned as a slave to one of the Prophet's Companions. That the Prophet, the leader of the Muslim community, chose her as a wife was an act of kindness that lightened her pain and compensated her for her loss. One of the Prophet's Companions was absolutely right when he said to the Prophet: 'Messenger of God, Ṣafiyyah bit Ḥuyay; [the daughter of] the chief of both Qurayẓah and al-Naḍīr, suits none other than you.'

A similar case was that of Juwayriyyah. She was also very pretty, and her father, al-Ḥārith, was the chief of his tribe, al-Muṣṭalaq. As a captive, she fell to one of the Prophet's Companions. She mentioned this to the Prophet and said: 'Messenger of God, I am Juwayriyyah bint al-Ḥārith, and what happened to me is not unknown to you. I have been allocated to Thābit ibn Qays ibn Shammās, but I have agreed terms to buy my freedom. I am here to seek your help in paying my price. The Prophet said to her: 'Would you consider a better offer?' She said: 'What offer, Messenger of God?' He said: 'I will pay for your freedom and marry you.' She said: 'I accept.' [Related by Abu Dāwūd]

That the Prophet, the leader of the Muslim community, chose her was an honour that removed her earlier humiliation when she became a captive. This act of honour by God's Messenger was crowned with a perfect ending. 'Ā'ishah narrated: 'When Muslims heard that the Prophet married Juwayriyyah, they freed the slaves of al-Muṣṭalaq tribe, saying that they could not enslave God's Messenger's in-laws.

We do not know of any woman who brought a greater blessing to her people. Through her, one hundred of al-Muṣṭalaq people were freed.'

Also in his companionship with his wives, the Prophet always aspired to that which is best. Were we to cite examples of this, we will give many, but we will confine our discussion to one example that gives a clear picture, as it aspires to what is most perfect.

'Ā'ishah narrated: "Hālah bint Khuwaylid, Khadījah's sister, sought permission to enter the Prophet's home. He recognized Khadījah's way of seeking permission. He said: 'My Lord, let it be Hālah.' I felt jealous and said: 'Why do you speak of an elderly Quraysh woman who lost her teeth and died many years ago, when God has given you one who is better?' (Another version related by Ahmad adds: 'God's Messenger (peace be upon him) said: God has not given me a better one than her. She believed in me when other people rejected my message. She believed me when others accused me of lying. She helped me with her wealth when others denied me.') [Related by al-Bukhari and Muslim]

'Ā'ishah reports: 'I was never more jealous of any one of the Prophet's wives than Khadījah, even though I never saw her. The Prophet, however, often mentioned her. He might slaughter a sheep and cut it into pieces and send them as gifts to Khadījah's friends. I said to him once: "As if there was no woman in the whole world other than Khadījah?" He said: "She was this, and she was that. She also gave me my children."' (In another version, the Prophet said: 'I was privileged with her love') [Related by al-Bukhari and Muslim]

'Ā'ishah narrated that a woman visited the Prophet (peace be upon him). A plate of meat was brought to him and he kept handing some of it to her. I said: 'Messenger of God, do not put your hand into it.' He said: ''Ā'ishah, this lady used to visit us during Khadījah's life. To be faithful to good times is a mark of faith.'

Aspiring to what is best in worship

Night worship: God says: 'You enfolded one! Stand in prayer at night, all but a small part of it, half of it, or a little less, or add to it. Recite the Qur'an calmly and distinctly. We shall bestow on you a weighty message. The night hours are strongest of tread and most upright of speech. During the day you have a long chain of things to attend to. Therefore, remember your Lord's name and devote yourself wholeheartedly to Him.' (73: 1-8)

'Ā'ishah narrated that God's Messenger (peace be upon him) used to pray during the night eleven *rak'ahs*. (Another version adds the following: You need not ask about their perfection and length.) He would stay in each prostration as long as any of you may take to recite 50 verses of the Qur'an before lifting his head. He would pray two *rak'ahs* before the obligatory Fajr Prayer, then lie down on his right side, until the caller came for the obligatory prayer.' [Related by al-Bukhari]

'Ā'ishah reports: 'One night I missed God's Messenger (peace be upon him) in bed. I reached for him and my hand touched the inside of his two feet as they were vertical [in prostration] in his praying place. He was saying: "My Lord, I seek shelter in Your pleasure from Your displeasure, and in Your pardon from Your punishment, and in You from You. I cannot praise You enough. All praise is Yours as You praise Yourself."' [Related by Muslim]

'Ā'ishah reports: 'The Prophet (peace be upon him) used to stand up in night worship until his feet split. I asked him: "Why do you do this, Messenger of God, when God has forgiven you your past and later sins?" He said: "Would I not love to be a grateful servant of God?" When he put on weight, he prayed sitting. Shortly before he wanted to bow [i.e. do the *rukū'*] he stood up, continued his recitation, then bowed.' [Related by al-Bukhari]

Ḥudhayfah said: 'One night I prayed with the Prophet (peace be upon him), and he started Surah 2, The Cow. I thought he would bow when he had recited 100 verses, but he went on. I thought that he would complete the surah in one *rak'ah*, but he went on. I then thought that he would bow when he had finished the surah. He then started Surah 4, Women and completed it, then he started Surah 3, Āl 'Imrān and completed it. He was reciting at ease. When he recited a verse that included God's glorification, he would glorify Him, and when he recited a verse with a supplication, he would say a supplication, and when he recited a prayer appealing for God's shelter, he would say the same. He then bowed and started repeating the phrase, "Limitless is my Supreme Lord in His glory." The length of his bow was close to the length of his [recitation] standing up. He then said: "May God respond to whoever praises Him," and he stood up for a long time, close to his bowing. He then prostrated himself and said: "Limitless is my Lord, the Most High in His glory." His prostration was close in length to his standing up.' [Related by Muslim]

'Ā'ishah said: '(When it was her night with God's Messenger), God's Messenger (peace be upon him) would go towards the end of the night to al-Baqīʿ and he would say: "Peace be to you, the dwellers of an abode of believing people. What you were promised for next day has come to you, certain to be at an appointed future time.[25] We, God willing, shall be joining you. My Lord, forgive the people of Baqīʿ al-Gharqad."' [Related by Muslim]

'Ā'ishah narrated: 'One night, when it was my turn for the Prophet to be with me, he came in, took off his garment, took off his sandals and placed them near the end of his bed and spread the edge of

25. The Prophet refers to what people are promised during their life to be coming, and that it is certain to happen when the time between death and resurrection is over.

his lower garment on his mattress and lay down. He stayed until he thought that I was fast asleep then he carefully put on his robe and sandals. He opened the door and went out, carefully closing the door. I put on my shirt, head dress and full dress and I then went out, following him. He reached al-Baqīʿ and stood there a long while then he raised his arms three times. He then turned and I turned. He walked fast and I walked fast; he jogged and I jogged; he ran and I ran. I was home ahead of him and went in. I had hardly laid down when he came in. He said: "What is wrong, ʿĀ'ish?[26] You are breathing so hard!" I said: "Nothing is wrong." He said: "You tell me, or I will be told by the One who knows all." I said: "Messenger of God, may my parents be sacrificed for you," and I told him. He said: "Then you were that blackness I saw in front of me?" I said: "Yes." He pushed me hard in my chest and hurt me. Then he said: "Did you think that God and His Messenger would be unfair to you?" I said: "Whatever people may conceal, God knows. Yes." He said: "Gabriel came to me when you saw. He called me, keeping that from you. I responded to him but did not tell you. He would not enter your room after you had taken off your clothes. When I thought that you were fast asleep, I did not want to wake you and I feared that you might feel lonely. He said to me: 'God commands you to go to al-Baqiʿ and pray for the forgiveness of those buried there.'" I asked: "What shall I say to them, Messenger of God?" He said: "Say: Peace be to the dwellers of this place who are believers and Muslims. May God bestow His Mercy on those of us who have gone ahead and those who are left behind. We shall certainly be joining you, God willing.'" [Related by Muslim]

Similarly, when he did his voluntary fasting, the Prophet aspired to what was best. Anas narrated: 'God's Messenger (peace be upon him) would not fast during a month until we might think that he would not be fasting at all in that month. He might also fast until we

26. The Prophet used a short form of her name.

might think that he would not abstain from fasting in that month. Whenever you wished to see him praying at night or asleep, you would certainly see him.' [Related by al-Bukhari]

Anas narrated: 'The Prophet continued fasting [into a second day] at the end of a certain month, and some people also continued fasting. The Prophet was informed. He said: 'Were the month to be extended for me, I would have remained fasting until those who go too far would stop. I am not like you. I continue to be given food and drink by my Lord.' In another version, the Prophet said: 'Do not continue fasting [into a second day].' Some people said: 'But you do.' He said: 'I stay the night when my Lord gives me to eat and drink. Do only what you can bear.' [Related by al-Bukhari and Muslim]

The prayer at the time of a solar eclipse is another manifestation of the Prophet's aspiration to perfection in matters of worship.

Asmā' said: 'The sun was eclipsed during God's Messenger's lifetime. I went into 'Ā'ishah's and found her praying. I said: "Why are people praying?" She pointed with her head to the sky. I said: "Is it a sign?" She signalled with her head meaning, "Yes." God's Messenger (peace be upon him) stood up for a very long time, and I was nearly fainting. (In a different version narrated by Muslim, Jābir ibn 'Abdullāh said: 'The sun went into eclipse during the Prophet's lifetime, on a very hot day. God's Messenger (peace be upon him) led his Companions in prayer, standing up for a long time, and some of them went down.') I took up a water bottle near me and I poured water over my head or on my face.'

(In another version related by Muslim, Asmā' said: 'He stayed in his standing position for a very long time so that I thought of sitting down. But then I might look at a weak woman and say to myself that this woman is weaker than me. I would then remain standing. He then bowed and stayed in the bowing position for a long time. He then raised his head and stood for a long time. Had a man come in then, he would think that [the Prophet] had not bowed yet.')

God's Messenger finished his prayer with the sun having been clear. He addressed the people, praising God and thanking Him. He then said: "Meanwhile..." She added: Some women from the Anṣār were talking, I turned to them to tell them to be quiet.' [Related by al-Bukhari and Muslim]

The Prophet's preference for simple living was another aspect of his aspiration to perfection and what is best. In this he fulfilled God's directive that he should not aspire to the luxuries of this world. God says: 'Do not turn your eyes covetously towards whatever splendour of this world's life We have allowed many of them to enjoy in order that We may test them thereby. Whatever provisions your Lord may give are indeed better and longer lasting.' (20: 131)

The Prophet (peace be upon him) did not care for any sort of life's luxury. He preferred what is simple and served the purpose. This was reflected in his diet and food preferences. 'Ā'ishah narrated: 'Muhammad's family never had their fill of wheat bread for three consecutive days from the time when he migrated to Madinah until he passed away.' [Related by al-Bukhari and Muslim]

Abu Ḥāzim said: 'I asked Sahl ibn Sā'idah: Did God's Messenger eat high quality wheat? Sahl said: "God's Messenger never saw high quality wheat from the day God gave him His message until He gathered his soul." I asked him whether they had sieves during the Prophet's lifetime. He said: "God's Messenger never saw a sieve from the first day of his message until his last day. I said: How could you eat barley without sifting it?" He said: "We used to grind it and then blow over it. Whatever is blown away is left out. The remainder is then watered and prepared to eat."' [Related by al-Bukhari]

ʿĀ'ishah, the Mother of Believers, said: 'God's Messenger (peace be upon him) came in one day and asked: "Do you have anything?" [He meant food] We said: No. He said: "Then I am fasting." He came in on another day and we said: Messenger of God, we have some *ḥays* [a dish made with dried milk, dates and butter]. He said: "Show it to me. I started the day fasting." He then ate of it.' [Related by Muslim]

Anas reported that the Prophet was brought some meat that was given as *ṣadaqah*, or charity, to Barīrah. He said: 'It is a charity to her, but to us it is a gift.'[27] [Related by Muslim]

In all aspects of life, the Prophet led a very simple way of life, managing with the bare essentials. Abu Burdah reported: 'I visited ʿĀ'ishah, and she brought us a thick lower garment which was of the type made in Yemen, and a cloak which people called 'patched up.' She swore by God that God's Messenger (peace be upon him) was wearing these two garments when he passed away.' [Related by al-Bukhari and Muslim. This is Muslim's version]

ʿĀ'ishah narrated: 'God's Messenger's mattress was made of hide and stuffed with fibre.' [Related by al-Bukhari and Muslim]

ʿAbdullāh said: 'God's Messenger (peace be upon him) slept on a straw mat. When he rose, its mark was clear on his side. We said: Messenger of God, let us bring you a soft mat. He said: "What do I care for this life. In this life I am just like a traveller who stopped in the shade of a tree then left it and went on his way."' [Related by al-Tirmidhī]

27. The point here is that the Prophet and his household are not allowed to take charity. As a poor person, Barīrah could have it because she did not belong to the Prophet's household. As she gave some of it to ʿĀ'ishah, it was a gift from her. Hence, the Prophet and his family could eat it.

‘Ā’ishah reported: ‘The Prophet (peace be upon him) passed away, and there was nothing on my shelf that may be eaten by anyone except an amount of barley.[28] I ate of it until I was bored with it.’ [Related by al-Bukhari and Muslim].

‘Amr ibn al-Ḥārith said: ‘The Prophet left nothing behind, except his arms, a white mule and a plot of land which he left to charity.’ [Related by al-Bukhari]

Anas reported that ‘he once took to the Prophet some barley bread and a sauce that had a changed smell... He heard the Prophet say: “This evening, Muhammad’s family do not have even one *ṣā‘* of wheat or grain.” He had nine wives at the time.’ [Related by al-Bukhari]

‘Ā’ishah reported: ‘When God’s Messenger (peace be upon him) passed away, his body armour was pawned with a Jew against thirty *ṣā‘s* of barley.’ [Related by al-Bukhari and Muslim]

The choice the Prophet offered his wives

God said: ‘Prophet! Say to your wives: “If you desire the life of this world and its charms, I shall provide for you and release you in a becoming manner; but if you desire God and His Messenger and the life of the Hereafter, know that God has readied great rewards for those of you who do good.”’ (33: 28-29)

Jābir ibn ‘Abdullāh reports: ‘Abu Bakr came to visit God’s Messenger (peace be upon him) and he found people sitting around near his home. None of them had been given permission to come in. Abu Bakr, however, was admitted and he went in. Then ‘Umar came over and sought permission to enter and he was admitted. He found the

---

28. It is said that she meant half of one *wasq*. A *wasq* is a measure equivalent to sixty *ṣā‘s*, and one *ṣā‘* is estimated at a little over two kilograms.

Prophet sitting down, silent and looking sad, with his wives around him. Abu Bakr thought: "I must say something to make the Prophet laugh." He said: "Messenger of God! I wish you had seen [my wife] Khārijah's daughter when she asked me for more money. I went up to her and poked her in the neck." God's Messenger (peace be upon him) smiled and said: "As you see, here they are asking me for more money." Abu Bakr went up to 'Ā'ishah [his daughter] to poke her in the neck, and 'Umar went up to Ḥafṣah [his daughter] to poke her in the neck. Each one of them said: "Are you asking God's Messenger what he does not have?" They said: "By God, we shall never ask God's Messenger what he does not have." The Prophet then stayed away from his wives for a month, or twenty-nine days.' [Related by Muslim]

'Umar ibn al-Khaṭṭāb narrated: 'I offered the Fajr Prayer with the Prophet (peace be upon him). He then went into an upstairs room and stayed alone... I went in and found God's Messenger (peace be upon him) reclining on a straw mat, which left its mark on his side. He was leaning on a pillow made of hide with fibre stuffing. I greeted him... I looked around in the Prophet's home and found nothing to satisfy the eye except for three sacks. I said: "Pray to God to give plentiful provisions to your community. The Persians and the Byzantines have been given plenty and yet they do not worship God." He was reclining, and said: "Are you in doubt, Ibn al-Khaṭṭāb? Those are peoples whose good things are given to them early in this present life." I said: "Messenger of God, pray to God to forgive me."

(In another version: I said: Have you divorced your wives? He said: No, but I am staying away from them for a month.) When twenty-nine days had passed, he entered 'Ā'ishah's room, beginning with her. 'Ā'ishah said to him: "You have sworn not to enter our homes for a month, and now we have passed twenty nine nights. I have counted them." The Prophet said: "This month is twenty-nine days." That month was indeed twenty-nine days.

'When God's Messenger (peace be upon him) was ordered to give his wives a choice, he started with me. He said: "I shall mention something to you, and you do not have to decide before you have consulted your parents." I said: I know that my parents would never tell me to part with you. He then said: "God, Mighty and Exalted, said: 'Prophet! Say to your wives: "If you desire the life of this world and its charms, I shall provide for you and release you in a becoming manner; but if you desire God and His Messenger and the life of the Hereafter, know that God has readied great rewards for those of you who do good."' (33: 28-29) I said: "Is this something on which I consult my parents? I choose God, His Messenger and the life of the Hereafter." The Prophet then offered the same choice to his other wives and they all said the same as 'Ā'ishah.' [Related by al-Bukhari and Muslim]

Special Privileges for Prophets: a Continuous and Miraculous Tradition

We will presently mention some of the texts related to the special privileges granted to Prophet Muhammad (peace be upon him) which are specifically concerned with sexual enjoyment. Before we do that, however, we need to make two observations. The first is that the special allowance provided to God's Messenger in the area of marriage and enjoyment is consistent with the overall perspective of Islamic law which gives people generally a broad area of permissibility. We discussed these in detail in Chapter 4 which deals with how Islam facilitates lawful ways of enjoying sexual pleasure. Prophets are given extra privileges that suit their roles and status.

The other observation is that what Prophet Muhammad was given was not unique in the history of God's prophets and messengers. God gave some of His prophets privileges that distinguished them. For example, Moses was given a large physical stature. Prophet Solomon was made a king and God gave him authority over the jinn, birds and wind, in addition to a miraculous sexual drive and strength. God says: 'No blame whatsoever attaches to the Prophet for doing what God has ordained for him. Such was God's way with those who went before him. God's will is always destiny absolute.' (33: 38)

The Prophet's hadiths mention some of Solomon's privileges. Abu Hurayrah narrated from the Prophet (peace be upon him): 'Sulaymān ibn Dāwūd [i.e. Solomon, son of David] said: "I shall consort tonight with seventy women, each of whom shall be pregnant with a fighter who shall fight for God's cause." His friend told him to say, "God willing," but he did not. (In a different version: he forgot.) He consorted with them, but none of them gave birth to a boy, except one who delivered half a boy.' [Related by al-Bukhari and Muslim]

The Prophet's special privileges in marriage and enjoyment

Let us remember first of all that the Prophet (peace be upon him) stated very clearly and frankly that he loved women. Anas narrated that God's Messenger (peace be upon him) said: 'What has been made appealing to me in this life of yours are women and perfume. But the dearest thing that gives me satisfaction is prayer.' [Related by Ahmad]

1. God Himself chooses some of the Prophet's wives

'Ā'ishah: The Prophet said to 'Ā'ishah: 'I was shown you twice in my sleep. I saw you wrapped in silk, and I was told, "This is your wife." I lifted the cover and I saw you. I thought, If this is from God, He will accomplish it.' [Related by al-Bukhari and Muslim]

Zaynab: God says: 'You did say to the one to whom God had shown favour and you had shown favour, "Hold on to your wife and have fear of God." And thus you would hide in your heart that which

God wanted to bring to light. You stood in awe of people, whereas it was God alone of whom you should have stood in awe. Then, when Zayd had come to the end of his union with her, We gave her to you in marriage, so that no blame should attach to the believers for marrying the spouses of their adopted sons when the latter have come to the end of their union with them. God's will must be fulfilled.' (33: 37)

2. A larger number of wives and exemption from some restrictions

God says: 'Prophet! We have made lawful to you the wives whom you have paid their dowries, as well as those whom God has placed in your right hand through war, as also the daughters of your paternal uncles and aunts, and the daughters of your maternal uncles and aunts, who have migrated with you; and any believing woman who offers herself freely to the Prophet and whom the Prophet might be willing to wed: [this latter] applies to you alone and not to other believers. We well know what We have made obligatory to them in respect of their wives and other women their right hands possess; and thus no blame shall attach to you. God is much-forgiving, ever-merciful.' (33: 50)

As for the privilege of having any number of wives, we know that when he passed away, the Prophet was married to nine wives: Sawdah, 'Ā'ishah, Ḥafṣah, Umm Salamah, Zaynab, Umm Ḥabībah, Juwayriyyah, Ṣafiyyah and Maymūnah. In addition, there were several proposed marriages which did not take place for various reasons that were not connected to number. We may look at some of these offers:

Umm Ḥabībah bint Abu Sufyān said: 'Messenger of God, marry my sister, Abu Sufyān's daughter?' 'He said: 'Would you like that?' I said: 'Yes, I am not your only wife, and the one I would love most to be my partner in all that is good is my sister.' He said: 'But she is unlawful to me.' I said: 'I am told that you have proposed to Durrah bint Abu Salamah.' He said: 'Umm Salamah's daughter?' I said: 'Yes.' He said: 'Had she not been my stepdaughter and foster child, she would still be unlawful to me. She is the daughter of my suckling brother. Abu Salamah and I were suckled by Thuwaybah. Therefore, do not propose to me your daughters or sisters.' [Related by al-Bukhari and Muslim]

'Alī said: 'Messenger of God, why do you go far to choose from the Quraysh and ignore us?' He said: 'Do you have any?' I said: 'Yes, Ḥamzah's daughter.' The Prophet said: 'She is unlawful to me; she is the daughter of my suckling brother.' [Related by Muslim]

Anas ibn Mālik said that some people said: 'Messenger of God, would you not marry a woman from the Anṣār?' He said: 'There is something in their eyes.' [Related by Ibn Ḥibbān]

Anas mentioned that a woman came to the Prophet and said to him: 'I have a daughter and would like to present her to you.' She described how pretty she was. The Prophet said: 'I accept her.' The woman continued to mention her daughter's merits, then said: 'She never had even a headache.' The Prophet said: 'I have no need of your daughter.' [Related by Ahmad]

There were also several marriage proposals: Abu Hurayrah narrated that the Prophet proposed to Umm Hāni' bint Abi Ṭālib. She said: 'Messenger of God, I have become old and I have children.' The Prophet said: 'The best women to ride camels are the good ones among the Quraysh women: they are the most caring of children when they are young, and the most considerate of husbands regarding their money.' [Related by Muslim]

Ibn 'Abbās narrated that the Prophet proposed to a woman from his own clan called Sawdah. She had five or six children by her deceased husband. She said to him: 'What stops me accepting is that you are the one I love most, but I want to spare you that these children may cry close to your head.' He said to her: 'May God bestow mercy on you. The best women to ride camels are the good ones among the Quraysh women.' [Related by Ahmad]

Jābir reported that the Prophet (peace be upon him) proposed to Umm Mubashshir bint al-Barā' ibn Ma'rūr. She said: 'I gave my [deceased] husband a pledge that I shall not marry anyone after him.' The Prophet said: 'This is not valid.' [Related by al-Ṭabarānī]

Moreover, the above quoted verse, 33:50, gives the Prophet an additional privilege, permitting him to accept any woman who makes of herself a gift to him, without paying any dowry. Several hadiths shed further light on this point: 'Ā'ishah said: 'I felt jealous of the women who gifted themselves to God's Messenger (peace be upon him), and I would say: "Would a woman make herself a gift?."' (Another version mentions: Khawlah bint Ḥakīm was one of those who offered themselves as gift to the Prophet.) [Related by al-Bukhari and Muslim]

Sahl ibn Sa'd reports that "a woman came to the Prophet and said: 'Messenger of God! I have come to make of myself a present to you.' The Prophet looked up and down at her several times, then he lowered his head. When the woman realized that the Prophet did not make a decision concerning her offer, she sat down." [Related by al-Bukhari and Muslim]

3. The Prophet was free how to divide his nights between his wives

God says [in a verse addressing the Prophet]: 'You may defer any of them you please, and take to yourself any of them you please. No blame will attach to you if you invite one whose turn you have previously set aside: this makes it more likely that they will be contented and not distressed, and that all of them will be satisfied with whatever you have to give them. God knows what is in your hearts. God is indeed all-knowing, clement.' (33: 51)

'Ā'ishah said that when God revealed the verse that says: 'You may defer any of them you please, and take to yourself any of them you please. No blame will attach to you if you invite one whose turn you have previously set aside,' I said [to the Prophet]: 'I see that your Lord gives you all that pleases you.' [Related by al-Bukhari and Muslim]

4. God gave a special honour to His Messenger, ordering his wives to be screened

God says: 'When you ask the Prophet's wives for something, do so from behind a screen: this makes for greater purity for your hearts and theirs.' (33: 53) Another aspect of honour God bestowed on His Messenger was that He made all his wives mothers, and their motherhood applies to all believers. God says: 'The Prophet has more claim on the believers than they have on their own selves; and his wives are their mothers.' (33: 6)

5. The special privilege that his wives would not marry anyone else

God says: 'Moreover, it does not behove you to give offence to God's Messenger, just as it would not behove you ever to marry his widows after he has passed away. That is certainly an enormity in God's sight.' (33: 53)

6. His privileges are total and permanent

This is reflected in two ways. The first is that no one can raise any objection to any privilege God has granted to His Messenger. He says: 'No blame whatsoever attaches to the Prophet for doing what

God has ordained for him.' (33: 38) The other aspect is seen in the fact that God disapproved of the Prophet denying himself something God has allowed him in order to please some of his wives. God says: 'Prophet, why do you prohibit yourself something that God has made lawful to you in your desire to please your wives? God is much-forgiving, ever-merciful. God has already ordained for you [believers] a way to release you from such oaths. God is your Lord Supreme. He alone is the All-Knowing, the Wise. The Prophet told something in confidence to one of his wives. When she divulged it, and God made this known to him, he spoke of a part of it and passed over a part. When he thus let her know of that, she asked, 'Who has told you this?' He said: 'The All-Knowing, the All-Aware told me.' Would that you two turn to God in repentance, for your hearts have swerved! But if you support each other against him, know that God is his protector, and that, therefore, Gabriel, all righteous believers and the angels will stand behind him.' (66: 1-4)

Anas mentions that God's Messenger had a slave woman with whom he consorted. 'Ā'ishah and Ḥafṣah continued to press him until he forbade himself that. God then revealed: "Prophet, why do you prohibit yourself something that God has made lawful to you in your desire to please your wives? God is much-forgiving, ever-merciful." (66: 1) [Related by al-Nasā'ī]

Then came a point when the Prophet's privilege to marry any women he wanted was stopped. God says: 'You [Muhammad] are not permitted to take any further wives, nor to exchange these for other wives, even though you are attracted by their beauty, except for any that your right hand may possess. God keeps watch over all things.' (33: 52)

How the Prophet Enjoyed Sex

When we look at any aspect of the Prophet's life, we need to bear in mind two important matters which will show that he followed the right way in whatever he did. This will enable us to have the correct understanding of the texts that speak about his approach to sexual enjoyment.

The first observation is that the Prophet's life was characterized by maintaining the right balance and complementarity between all his affairs. This is coupled with fair distribution of his responsibilities and the time he allocated for each. We should also bear in mind that God wants us to follow the Prophet's example in all matters, as he says: 'In God's Messenger you have a good model for everyone who looks with hope to God and the Last Day.' (33: 21) This means that we must cast a comprehensive look at the Prophet's life, considering all its aspects. We must not concentrate on any particular aspect, because an imbalanced outlook will only lead to deficient understanding, followed by a faulty conception of his conduct.

A person who monitors how the Prophet attended to his worship and follows its various forms is bound to think that worship was his only concern. If one studies his military activity and expeditions, he will conclude that he was a warrior who devoted himself to fighting his enemies and sending one military expedition after another. Yet, when we look at how he taught his Companions and instructed them in all their affairs, including minor ones, we imagine that all his time and effort were consecrated for this purpose. And when we reflect on how he took care of his Companions, visiting the young and old, accepting their invitations, feeding the hungry, helping the weak, enquiring about those who are absent, receiving visitors, blessing their newborns, visiting the sick and leading the prayer for their dead, we feel that such caring attention to his community was his top priority. Finally, when we look at the Prophet's love of the women in his household, his loving care of his wives and his lovemaking we may think that there was no room in his heart for anyone other than women.

Therefore, when we cite how the Prophet enjoyed himself with his wives we should bear in mind how he attended to his worship, conducted his jihad, taught his Companions and took care of them, in addition to how he managed the affairs of the fledgeling Islamic state. Only with such a comprehensive vision can we formulate a correct understanding of the Prophet and his life.

The other observation which helps in clarifying the Prophet's conduct in his life is that a person with strong feelings always expresses his emotions generously. When such emotions apply to a particular wife and express itself in sexual pleasure, it will not be a purely physical pleasure. The enjoyment is only one of its aspects which include love, respect, tenderness and even consolation. These are noble feelings that may sometimes be expressed with a kiss or a tender touch.

We will now cite texts that mention some of the Prophet's practices in enjoying sexual pleasure. Most of these texts have been mentioned in the previous chapters, but we now put them together, in summarized form to highlight the Prophet's approach to enjoying sex. Our other purpose is to make clear that these practices are permissible to all believers. They are not special privileges of the Prophet. We should remember that his normal practice is natural human practice. Thus, he shares with all believers their love of women, and his conduct with his wives is the right and natural one.

Quick visits in the morning, afternoon and evening

Ibn ʿAbbās narrated: 'When God's Messenger (peace be upon him) finished Fajr Prayer, he stayed in his place with people around him until sunrise. He then visited his wives, one by one, greeting them and supplicating for them. When it was any one's day, he stayed with her.' [Related by Ibn Mardawayh]

‘Ā’ishah reported: ‘When God’s Messenger (peace be upon him) finished the ‘Aṣr Prayer, he visited his wives, and he would be close to them.’ [Related by al-Bukhari and Muslim]

‘Ā’ishah said: ‘God’s Messenger did not favour any of us in how he divided his time with us. Rarely a day passed without him visiting us all. He would draw close to each woman, without physical contact.’ (In a version related by al-Bayhaqī: He would kiss and touch, but not have intercourse.) When he reached the one whose day it was, he would stay the night with her.’ [Related by Abu Dāwūd]

Anas narrated: ‘The Prophet (peace be upon him) had nine wives. When he divided his nights between them, he would return to the first one on the ninth night. They would meet every evening in the home of the one where the Prophet would stay that night. Once he was in ‘Ā’ishah’s home. Zaynab came in and he stretched his hand to her. She [meaning ‘Ā’ishah] said: “This is Zaynab.” The Prophet withdrew his hand.’ [Related by Muslim]

Drawing lots to decide whom to take on a journey

‘Ā’ishah narrated the following story when the people of falsehood circulated whatever they did about her. She said: ‘God’s Messenger (peace be upon him) drew lots between us as he was about to travel. Whoever was drawn out would be in his company. Once as he was going on a military expedition, he drew lots between us and it came out in my favour. I went with God’s Messenger (peace be upon him) after the screening was made obligatory. I was carried and put down in my howdah....’ [Related by al-Bukhari and Muslim]

‘Ā’ishah narrated: ‘When the Prophet intended to travel, he drew lots between his wives. On one occasion, the draw came out in favour of ‘Ā’ishah and Ḥafṣah. When it was night, the Prophet would march alongside ‘Ā’ishah and conversed [with her]. Ḥafṣah said [to ‘Ā’ishah]:

"Would you like to ride my camel tonight and I ride yours: you will be looking around and I will?" She said: "Yes." I rode her camel. The Prophet came to 'Ā'ishah's camel when Ḥafṣah was riding it. He greeted her and marched until they stopped for rest. He only then missed 'Ā'ishah. When they dismounted, she put her feet in the *idhkhar* plant and said: 'My Lord, let a scorpion or a snake bite me, but I could not say anything to him.' [Related by al-Bukhari and Muslim]

Kissing in all situations

'Ā'ishah narrated that the Prophet kissed one of his wives then went out to offer the prayer without performing a fresh ablution. [Related by al-Tirmidhī]

'Ā'ishah narrated: 'The Prophet (peace be upon him) used to kiss his wife and play with her while fasting, but he was the one who controlled his desire best.' [Related by al-Bukhari and Muslim]

'Ā'ishah narrated: 'When any of us [the Prophet's wives] was having her period, and the Prophet wanted to be intimate with her, he would tell her to cover herself with her lower garment, when she was at the height of her period, then he would be close with her.' [Related by al-Bukhari and Muslim]

Going to one's wife after seeing a woman. Jābir reports that God's Messenger (peace be upon him) saw a woman, and he went to his wife Zaynab as she was dying a piece of leather. He had with her whatever he wanted. He then came out....' [Related by Muslim]

Before and after ihram

'Ā'ishah narrated: 'I applied perfume to God's Messenger (peace be upon him), then he went around to his wives. He then started his consecration in the morning.' [Related by al-Bukhari and Muslim]

'Ā'ishah narrated: 'We performed the hajj with the Prophet (peace be upon him) and we performed the *ṭawāf* of *ifāḍah* on the Day of Sacrifice. Then Ṣafiyyah started her period. The Prophet wanted with her what a man wants with his wife. I said: "Messenger of God, she is in menstruation." He said: "Will she be detaining us?" They said: "Messenger of God, she performed the *ṭawāf* of *ifāḍah* on the Day of Sacrifice." He said: "Let us go."' [Related by al-Bukhari and Muslim].

Repeated intercourse

'Ā'ishah narrated: 'The Prophet (peace be upon him) might have intercourse, then do it again without performing the ablution in between.' [Related by al-Ṭaḥāwī]

Abu Rāfiʿ narrated that the Prophet visited his wives on the same night, taking a bath at this one's place and that one's place. [Related by Abu Dāwūd]

Taking a bath with his wife

Umm Salamah said: 'I used to take a bath with the Prophet taking water from the same container, to remove our state of ceremonial impurity.' [Related by al-Bukhari and Muslim]

Waiting a long time to do compensatory fasting

Yaḥyā narrated from Abu Salamah. He said: I heard 'Ā'ishah say: 'I might owe some fasting from Ramadan, but could not do the compensatory fasting until Shaʿbān.'[29] Yaḥyā said: 'What prevented her was attending to the Prophet's needs.' [Related by al-Bukhari and Muslim]

---

29. Shaʿbān is the month that precedes Ramadan in the lunar calendar. The hadith means that the Prophet's wives would delay doing their compensatory fasting in order to attend to the Prophet's needs. But when they were in Shaʿbān they could not delay it any longer.

ʿĀ'ishah narrated: 'Any one of us might not fast in Ramadan during the Prophet's lifetime, yet might also not be able to do her compensatory fasting in God's Messenger's presence until we were in Shaʿbān. (In another version: because of God's Messenger's needs.) [Related by Muslim]

Gifting one's day

ʿĀ'ishah narrated: 'The Prophet used to allocate to each one of his wives her day and night. Sawdah bint Zamʿah gifted her day and night to ʿĀ'ishah, the Prophet's wife, to please God's Messenger (peace be upon him).' [Related by al-Bukhari]

ʿĀ'ishah said: 'I have never known a woman whom I would love to be like better than Sawdah bint Zamʿah. She was a sharp woman. When she grew old, she gifted her turn with God's Messenger to ʿĀ'ishah. She said: "Messenger of God, I give my day with you to ʿĀ'ishah." Subsequently, God's Messenger used to assign two days to ʿĀ'ishah: her own day and Sawdah's day.' [Related by Muslim]